CONNECT
with your
KIDS
for a
LIFETIME

DENA S. BOSWELL

OLIVER
NELSON

THOMAS NELSON PUBLISHERS

Nashville • Atlanta • London • Vancouver

Published in Nashville, Tennessee, by Thomas Nelson, Inc., Publishers, and distributed in Canada by Word Communications, Ltd., Richmond, British Columbia.

The Bible version used in this publication is THE NEW KING JAMES VERSION. Copyright © 1979, 1980, 1982, 1990, Thomas Nelson, Inc., Publishers.

Library of Congress Cataloging-in-Publication Data

Boswell, Dena S., 1949–
    Connect with your kids for a lifetime / Dena S. Boswell.
      p.   cm.
    ISBN 0-7852-8170-3 (pbk.)
      1. Parent and child.   2. Play.   3. Parenting.   I. Title.
    HQ755.85.B68   1995
    649'.1—dc20   95-11826
                                                                 CIP

Printed in the United States of America.

1 2 3 4 5 6 — 00 99 98 97 96 95

To my dear mother, whose creativity and playfulness formed lasting memories in my childhood. To my precious husband, Andrew, and our seven beautiful children, Ruth, David, Sarah, Esther, Hannah, Jonathan, and Deborah, whose love and encouragement made possible the writing of this book. Above all, to the gracious Lord, who instilled these creative ideas in my heart in the first place.

CONTENTS

Part Four: Creative Games for Adult and Child to Play

Conclusion: Connect Hearts for a Lifetime

FOREWORD

As I am reviewing *Connect with Your Kids for a Lifetime,* I am preparing a seminar on childhood depression. A number of children suffer from the often silent pain of this emotional illness.

If the message of this excellent book were practiced, childhood depression could be cured! The creative play Dena Boswell describes is a prescription for healthy family bonding through shared fun.

What a lovely blueprint for happiness this book is!

Grace Ketterman, M.D.
Author of *Parenting the Difficult Child*

PREFACE

Connecting with your child for a lifetime is a work of art. As creative expression often produces a masterpiece in the artistic world, so creative communication may produce a masterpiece in family relations. Playful creativity is one form of communication common to children, and adults need to master speaking this endearing and fascinating language.

The words of creative communication may be near the surface of an adult's consciousness just waiting to be remembered and used. Within every grown man there still lives a little boy and within every grown woman lives a little girl. The past playful creativity peeks out from behind the grown-up exterior and whispers, "I'm still here. Remember me!"

Connecting with your child more easily occurs when you learn how to appropriately shed any inappropriately grown-old ways of thinking, speaking, and acting and tenderly touch the heartstrings of the child. By mastering the language of playful creativity, you will more effectively communicate to your child and establish a more meaningful relationship.

To you, the adult reader, may you learn how to become like a child again.

ACKNOWLEDGMENTS

To my good friend Nancy King, who gave me ideas along the way and a summer retreat to creatively write. To the Coral Ridge Presbyterian Church Young Mothers' Group, whose interest and encouragement helped express many of these concepts. To family members and friends, whose prayers and love have sustained me while writing.

Part 1

Creative Play
Is a Language
of the Heart

Their hearts may be encouraged,
being knit together in love.
—Colossians 2:2

CHAPTER 1

The Language of Creative Play

"**D**addy! Daddy! Do it again!" squeals Billy with delight. "Rrrummm! Zzzooommm! Tower to Billy, Circle one more time, then lower legs for landing," says the father, holding his laughing three–year–old secure in strong arms. He whirls once more as Billy pretends to be a soaring plane high overhead.

The thrill and wonder the child feels. The youthful endearment the parent experiences. In this playful game, the parent and the child share more than a brief moment of fun. A bridge of communication is subtly being built, which will help prevent in coming years the distant, threatening silence between loved ones who have grown into strangers.

Heartfelt communication between parent and child does not mysteriously happen. It is the rewarded effort of the parent who knowingly or even unknowingly attempts to bridge the barriers that block good communication.

One thing basic to effective communication is expressing yourself in a manner understandable to the listener. At the level of understanding and being understood you need to be creative. You *want* to reach your child's heart, but you need tangible ways to do so.

All parents face the natural dilemma of trying to bridge the age gap. As parent and child try to interact, each seems to be speaking a different language. Probably, that is exactly what is happening.

Both parent and child hear and understand each other's words, and the parent usually gets the audible meaning of the child's speech. But the child's heart messages interwoven within verbal communication and nonverbal body language express the child's inner feelings, thoughts, and emotions about self and the world. The parent needs to hear and understand more with the heart.

The adult often hears only the words the child speaks and seldom understands and responds to the messages that the child's heart expresses through verbal and nonverbal language. Although a child is especially creative and adept at a wide range of expressive communication, communicative abilities surface in play.

Play Communicates

Children may communicate through playful activity to varying degrees. Some children are naturally more creative and expressive than others. However, most children are much more playfully expressive than most grown-ups, who generally have outgrown many playful tendencies. This depletion of youthful expression effectively shuts down much of the meaningful communication that could otherwise be shared between parent and child.

Learning how to *speak* the language of creative play and to imaginatively *use* it to connect with your child is the purpose of this book. You have at your fingertips the means to do this. You have the ability to communicate to your child's inner being and sound the depths of your child's heart. Through creative play, you are given the unique opportunity to speak to your youngster in a language the child understands and loves.

Two Kinds of Play

Playful activity basically occurs in two forms—structured and creative. Both forms communicate; however, one is decisively more powerful and imaginative.

Structured Play

Structured play is by far the more prevalent and widely practiced of the two. It may be highly competitive and professional in nature. The umpire bellows, "Play ball!" and the Little League baseball game begins. Or structured play may be fun activities or exercise. The children jumping rope on the sidewalk chant, "One, two, buckle my shoe; three, four, shut the door."

Structured play includes sports, such as baseball, football, and basketball, programmed/board games such as Nintendo, Monopoly, and Candyland, and simple fun events, such as jump rope, hopscotch, and marbles. Regardless of the game's complexity or intensity, set rules govern the proper way to play.

A child's unique personality is confined within the boundary of the rules. Children allowed the imaginative expression to discard rules governing structured games would cause chaos. A coach could say, "Sure, guys, make a touchdown at either end of the football field," or "Why not touch third base first when you're making a home run?"

Structured play tends to capitalize on a person's physical skill, natural talent, or mental prowess to successfully engage in or win the game. If the imagination is used, it helps win the competitive game or fun activity.

Without doubt, structured play is extremely beneficial to the physical, mental, and social development of a child, and it should be encouraged and practiced. It enables a child to gain skills, knowledge, and self-confidence. Through structured play, the child triumphantly says, "I can do it!"

As beneficial as structured play is, do not dismiss the importance of creative play. So, what exactly is creative play, and how does it differ from structured play?

Creative Play

Creative play, far more than structured play, engages the imagination. Have you ever watched the touch football game Dad is trying to play with his daughters disintegrate into a chase through the mud? Or the mother's intended cutout cookie dough becomes rolled snake-shaped creations under little helping hands? Structured games and activities that started out so well suddenly are displaced, rules thrown to the wind, by a playful abandonment to creative fun. Whimsical foolishness? Perhaps—or perhaps something deeper is being communicated.

Often, the imaginative playful creativity of an individual is surfacing and breathing the fresh air of expression. Something profound is being communicated through creative play. What is this unique form of communicating at which most children are masters?

Creative play is the natural childlike ability to express one's personality, feelings, and attitudes with imaginative words and actions. It is play that focuses on having fun and sharing in a relationship by using the imagination. A person's original ideas are given a springboard through playful activity, and self-expression is allowed to take off.

The person's ability to make believe adventures, activities, or events—not game rules—sets the limits of the game. Participants win by playing with imagination rather than by competing successfully against each other. A person's skill, strength, intelligence, or age is of no consequence. When true creative play occurs between an adult and a child, the child is equal in every way to the grown-up. In fact, the child is often the leader in the activity.

For most children, creative play is a built-in ability. It is an outward form of expressing their creative thoughts and inward feelings.

Is creative play childish or childlike? What are the differences? We will look at both in chapter 6, but first let's see why creative play is used so little.

If Creative Play Is So Natural, Why Is It Used So Little?

"I want to watch more cartoons!" begs the five-year-old transfixed before the television as his mother turns off the set and hurries him out the front door. The family's active Saturday continues with the child's soccer practice at ten o'clock, an older sister's gymnastics class at two, and a national football play-off game at four.

If creative play is a natural and meaningful form of communicating, why would one miss enjoying it? Time set aside for leisure and relaxation may include so much electronic entertainment, structured activities, and spectator sports that a person's free hours are consumed by these enjoyable pursuits.

Another subtle reason may be the modern adult's and child's loss of imagination and creativity of expression when they are playing. Leisure playtime for grandparents probably meant a broomstick for a horse, a blanket for a tent, and mud pies for a meal.

Playtime for today's children involves many toys that are three-dimensional copies of the screen creations produced by the entertainment media. Observe the stuffed animals, action figures, or games in department stores which encourage children to mimic the fanciful ideas, interesting story line, or creative action seen in the movie. The child's innate creativity may become secondary to the creative thinking of another.

Perhaps the enormous imbalance of structured over creative play is due largely to the disuse of imaginative thinking. Creative play is fueled by an active imagination, and it engages and ignites a dormant imagination. Creative play helps to get the imagination started, and it helps to keep it running well.

Though creative play is far more expressive than structured play, either can be exhausting and counterproductive. Most parents want to be involved in their child's life, and the youngster's playful tendencies offer a natural means in which to engage him in the relationship. However, trying to satisfy a child's selfish demand for attention by participating in his play can be damaging to both parent and child.

When Tommy incessantly clamors, "Mommy, Mommy, push me again!" when he pleads to be lifted for the third time into the swing just as his tired mother is comfortably settled on the park bench to nurse her infant daughter, an imbalance exists. The question of engaging in further play, whether structured or creative, is irrelevant. An exhausted parent coerced to perform or a demanding child extracting indulgent attention from a parent offers a poor incentive to repeat playful communication in the future.

In creative play, the activity is not too wearing, lengthy, or tedious. Quickly discontinue it if it is. To connect with your child, wisely set healthy boundaries of involvement and reasonable time limits. This is essential if you intend for play, whether structured or creative, to be a powerful bonding force in the relationship with your child.

Creative Play Is for Adults

"Daddy, let me have a turn now," pleads a young son as he impatiently waits for his daddy to stop playing with his electric toy train on Christmas morning.

"Oh! Look at those adorable miniatures!" exclaims the woman shopping at the craft store. She pauses to carefully handle the replica antique doll furniture on display.

She and the pajama-clad father are reliving a memory or fascination from childhood almost as if the little child from within is peeking out from behind the grown-up exterior. The very fact that most adults love to relive a dear feeling, fascination, or memory from childhood indicates how profound that creative, playful moment in the past was. It shows how great an impact was made on the heart. Like an old friend from the past revisiting, there is something wonderfully familiar and good about playing like a kid again.

However, most adults seldom allow the child inside to get out and express itself. Sharing in a playful romp or a make-believe tea party with their youngsters would do them a world of good. Life can be experienced on the lighter side when playfully engaging children in a creative, enjoyable way.

Beyond this wholesome emotional release, something profoundly deep occurs in the relationship. A clear line of communication between adult and child is being forged. Creative play is like a special language all in itself. The child easily communicates inner feelings and emotions by it, and he readily understands ideas and concepts that the adult conveys to him through it.

You may need to become more adept at communicating with your child in this language form and on your child's level. What can you do? Recognize creative play is a language of the heart and then learn how to speak it!

Creative Play Is a Language of the Heart

Creative play evidences itself as an ageless, universally known language by which humans express their thoughts and feelings. Even the very young speak it. "I'll be Mommy and you be Daddy," declares the three-year-old to her playmate, and they pretend to be grown-ups. Older people express it. "Horsey, horsey rides to town. Horsey, horsey don't fall down," says Grandpa to his toddler grandchild on his knee. In creative play, the generations meet, sharing fun on the common ground of make-believe, and the mutual bond of love is strengthened.

Creative play is a universal form of communicating because it is a language of the heart. It is heart art, and as with all true art, creative expression in the medium and method will convey a meaningful message to others.

The Medium of Creative Play

The primary medium consists of words, intonation, body movement, and facial expressions. For instance, a mother wanting to build a closer relationship with her young son can use the medium of her expressive mannerisms to weave a fascinating make-believe adventure. To have fun and draw her son closer, she can engage in creative play and at the same time communicate a deep sense of love and acceptance to him.

The Make-Believe Train Ride

The mother says, "I'm going on a train ride. Want to come?" She makes an unusual suggestion, and she captures the child's interest.

She mysteriously whispers the invitation to her young son. Then she pats the soft cushion of the couch, motioning him to cuddle up beside her. With a big smile and eyes twinkling, she pretends to hold the controls with one hand and pull a train whistle with the other.

"Chooo. Chooo. Chooo. I do love train rides, don't you?" she says. Then conducting the make-believe train through countryside and cities before arriving safely back home in time for milk and cookies, the mother easily spellbinds her young son for ten minutes.

The mother used her imagination, her body, and the living room couch to create the adventure. She spoke words to welcome her young son, her intonation dramatized the adventure, her body movement embraced him, and her facial expression was animated.

As important as the medium is to creative play, the method is even more important. The child's imagination can easily adjust to a lack of props in a make-believe adventure. However, no amount of imagination on the child's part can overcome the adult's disinterested or uncreative method in handling the materials.

The Method of Creative Play

The method must employ creative expression to communicate to the heart. The method takes the human body and common objects and uses them in a creative fashion. For instance, in the make-believe train ride the mother used her eyes, voice, arms, and legs as well as the couch in an imaginative manner.

To successfully capture a child's interest and imagination, the method of expressing the medium must be captivating. It is pointless for the adult to use his body or objects with lifeless gestures or involvement and expect his child to be intrigued.

The way in which the adult carries out this method of being creative is limitless. For instance, the mother could have just as easily imagined the couch as a circus train filled with exotic animals. She could have encouraged her young son to run quickly to his bedroom, gather up his teddy bear, blanket, and other stuffed animals, hop on the train with them, and become the fearless animal trainer who takes his three-ring circus by freight car to cities far and wide. What unusual happenings could the mother and the child imagine and develop along the way?

The intent of a creative and imaginative method is always to use your ideas, your body, and common objects to weave a make-believe adventure that spellbinds your child. What an unusual way of identifying with your youngster and communicating a real sense of enjoying each other's presence!

When you learn to use the medium of yourself in a creative and imaginative method, you convey vital messages to the heart of your child. What are some of these messages? Some of the most basic are love, friendship, and acceptance. Let's look at how creative play speaks to the heart of a child with these words: "I love you"; "Let's be friends"; and "Listen to me."

Three Vital Heart Messages of Creative Play

"I Love You"

"I love you" is the most significant message. You must communicate love in tangibly felt ways to give your child a sense of security and self-worth.

Creative play enables you to communicate in a relational manner. Your child hears "I love you" loud and clear as you make room in your grown-up world. You give your child time, energy, attention, and *yourself* by opening up your unique personality for viewing on your child's level.

Incorporating the childlike qualities of spontaneity, imagination, and activity in your interaction enables your child to emotionally hear the message. You express affection and love to your child by personally identifying with that child.

"Let's Be Friends"

"Let's be friends" needs to be genuinely impressed on the heart and mind of the child. You communicate this message when you willingly position your child on an equal basis with yourself in a game, sharing a partnership of fantasy. Though structured play allows a parent and a child to be team players participating together in an activity, the sense of equal position and camaraderie distinguishes creative play as a more effective communicator of friendship.

You are saying, "I want to be like you," when you creatively play with childlike spontaneity and imagination. Best friends have a way of thinking like each other, behaving like each other, and becoming like each other in various ways and degrees. You communicate your desire to be best friends when you willingly imitate positive childlike qualities and when you place your child on an equal basis with yourself.

"Listen to Me"

"Listen to me" is best communicated while you are having fun with your child. Creative play enables your child to more readily listen to, believe, and embrace the heart message you are attempting to communicate. Why? The child's heart is motivated to reason, *I will listen to you because I feel that you are my best friend who loves me.*

You encourage this heart response by closely identifying with what your child closely identifies. Your child identifies with creative playing and with the attitude of playfulness, so when you skillfully interact with both, you capture your child's interest and attention.

Creative play facilitates the child's ability to listen to messages of love and friendship and be affected by them. By identifying with your child, you are saying, "I am like you."

The New Testament writer Paul understood and implemented this principle of identification in his sharing the gospel. Paul stated, "To the Jews I became as a Jew, that I might win Jews. . . . I have become all things to all men, that I might by all means save some" (1 Cor. 9:19–22). Paul "becoming as" his listeners readied their hearts to receive his life-giving message.

In regard to creative play, the purpose of an adult becoming as a child is to open a channel of communication that reaches a child's heart and helps to establish a significant relationship. Yet too many adults and children find little time to creatively communicate in an imaginative and fun manner. What keeps adults and children from interacting in creative play?

Prowling Play Killers

This form of communication is like an endangered species. It is being crowded out by the hostile environment of sophisticated toy gadgetry and hunted to near extinction by prowling play killers of our culture. These toys indulge children in busyness and activity; they don't engage imagination in creative play. And the prowling play killers are known by the *too* in their names.

Too Busy

"I'll come see your fort later," calls the mother mopping her kitchen floor. "I want to watch more cartoons!" pleads the youngster. People are *too busy* to engage in playful creativity. Little time is left for the adult to spontaneously romp with the kids or for the child to imagine himself an explorer in a make-believe jungle on the back porch. The child is too preoccupied to create, and the adult is too busy to notice. Both are too distracted to pause and enjoy a playful and creative relationship.

Too Tired

"No! Not right now. Maybe later. OK, Honey?" abruptly responds the weary young father stretched out in his favorite chair. Hiding behind the evening newspaper, he tries to ignore his little daughter hugging her storybook beside him. He is *too tired* to think, let alone participate in sharing a few brief moments of endearment. Many times the adult emotionally feels this way whether the physical exhaustion is real or imaginary.

Too Stressed

"Sure, Son! Tomorrow we'll play catch. I gotta run now." And the time seldom comes when Dad is really there for his child. *Too stressed* with other matters of life, the parent forgets to take precious moments to build a lasting relationship in the heart and memory of his child. The urgent demands of the adult world drain the interest and excitement from engaging in any playful activity. Time and time again the youngster asks the adult to become a part of his childhood. Time and time again the grown-up is too stressed out and refuses. Finally, the child gives up and stops asking. The parent even then is too stressed to realize what wonderful opportunities he has missed in shaping a relationship with his youngster.

Too Old-Spirited

"No! Jill, you can't make a fort in the living room with the sheets and pillows!" declares the impatient mother whose rigid sense of order refuses to budge, even though her child's rainy day cabin fever threatens to bounce her off the walls. She is *too old-spirited* to creatively engage a child's interest, industry, and originality with anything better than television or a video game when times of boredom occur. Adults are at great risk of burying their own and their children's expressive abilities, leaving little energy or interest to be truly creative.

Too Afraid

"Really, I don't think I can be a very good horsey, Sweetheart," fumbles Dad as he uncomfortably tries to excuse himself from the children's enactment of the stagecoach robbers' getaway.

Viewing their make-believe games as a spectator is adequate and comfortable; becoming involved as an active participant, he feels *too afraid*. Some adults imagine themselves as having little or no ability in becoming playfully creative with their children. Often, they would rather be distant and disengaged than attempt anything that might appear amateurish or out of character from their familiar parental role.

It is time for adults to arrest the prowling play killers and engage in relational activities that tap the reservoirs of creativity. The play killers must be stopped before they drain the pleasure and wholesome fun from the very relationships that should be characterized by vital communication.

You Can Do It!

Adults must experience how wonderfully fun and easy it is to creatively play with their youngsters. Learning to speak this unique language of children will tremendously help parents in capturing children's hearts and in winning children over to a more loving relationship.

Creative play is a skill you can master. You can tailor it to fit your personality and disposition. More important than the activity is your mind-set to engage in genuine playfulness and youthful expression. There is wide diversity of personal creativity in this area, and your background and temperament will significantly shape your sense of appropriate behavior and your comfort zone of playfulness. Chapter 2 takes a look at the art of creative play and reveals underlying principles and guidelines.

The Creative Art
of Make-Believe

"**Y**ou're eating her nose! And her ears, too!" exclaims the mother to her daughter in the high chair. The child's plate of food is decorated with colorful carrot curls around the rim for hair; triangular-cut finger sandwiches in the middle for mouth, nose, and eyes; and a peach half on each side for ears.

The face on the plate has a roguish similarity to the red-haired girl. Picking up one of the small triangular shapes, the child proudly begins eating her peanut butter-and-jelly sandwich. Then poking the juicy peach with her finger, she giggles and impishly takes a big bite of the peach, too.

The mother pretends to plead for her daughter to be gentle while gobbling up the pretty plate face girl. The mother mimics a high-pitched voice as if the plate is talking: "Please, please eat me gently, little girl! Ohhh, I'm disappearing. Help!"

This touch of make-believe only animates and heightens the child's interest and appetite. A child's routine lunchtime has become a creative and playful adventure in eating.

The wise parent will attempt to weave this kind of activity into the fabric of the child's life. Why? Because children *do* pretend. Children create intrigue, fantasy, and make-believe adventures of their own. The adult who joins in the fun is speaking to the heart in a way the child knows, loves, and understands.

You may think, *Be imaginative! How can I be good at that?* Think back to the invisible playmate of your childhood. Remember the fun and exploits? Perhaps you gave your pretend friend a name. If you did not have a make-believe friend as a child, most likely you remember someone who did. The invisible playmate would carry on conversations only the child could hear. Schemes were invented; harmless mischief was carried out with the secret playmate. Of course, the child's make-believe pal was the one who really nibbled up the second graham cracker!

The invisible playmate of childhood is only one of the many examples of creative make-believe a child should experience during the formative years. Normal and wholesome fantasies develop and inspire a young person's creativity and imagination. Both are precious qualities and are in short supply in our culture.

Entertaining an invisible playmate or having imaginative adventure is *not* to be confused with involvement in the occult. Spiritual wickedness is a real and destructive force; delving into the spirit world of evil is totally opposite to developing the spirit of imaginative, playful creativity. It is vital parents know the vast difference between wholesome childlike fantasy and exploration of the occult.

Creative play is not destructive in any way. However, a child may become so engrossed with an imaginative exploit that his play appears destructive. By nature, children are imaginative, and it is little wonder that healthy imagination spills over into playful fantasy and sometimes mischievous predicaments.

The old battered cardboard box Tommy found behind the drugstore soon becomes a ship sailing out to sea. Finally crumpled flat from the long and reckless voyage, it becomes the slippery deck of a shipwrecked vessel by soaking it down with the garden hose. Just as the cardboard becomes soggy and disintegrated and a six-foot-square patch of backyard is a muddy mess, Tommy's mother opens the kitchen door to call him for supper.

Become a Master of Make-Believe

How can you learn to behave creatively? Learn to master the skills of inventing make-believe games.

Chapter 1 briefly discussed creative play and a make-believe game. This chapter will look at both in detail. What makes up a make-believe game? What is this building block of creative play?

The General Anatomy of Make-Believe Games

Playful creativity has the common thread of make-believe games running through its entire fabric. Playful and creative thoughts, words, and actions originate from a person's unique imagination. Here at the imaginative level many adults need prompting to jump-start their make-believe ability.

The process is relatively simple. Once you catch the spirit of make-believe games, your inner youthfulness will carry you along in a manner compatible with your personality. Again, the secret of good make-believe is to allow that little child out in free and wholesome expression.

Are Make-Believe Games Structured or Creative Play?

The two broad categories of play are structured and creative. Distinctions exist between the two; however, blending may occur. Blending structured into creative is more easily done than merging creative into structured. The very nature of structured play restricts the imaginative element. Yet an adult and a child may throw structured play to the wind, creatively playing an activity by abandoning the characteristics of structured play.

The Basic Elements of Structured Play

Prescribed Rules

Structured play has prescribed game rules which range from minimal to extensive and emphasize that participants follow a plan of logic, skill, or strategy. The rules allow a person to enhance his ingenuity and maneuverability.

Learning to follow game rules is an excellent and enjoyable way for children to develop self-discipline and concentration in completing tasks. Prescribed game rules offer good and fair boundaries by which participants learn to control themselves and their behavior.

However, game rules may limit creative imagination. How? After all the energy, effort, and concentration spent by the player's focusing on winning, there is little time or interest left to make believe.

Ability

Structured play majors on a person's ability or skilled strength, agility, or quick reflex to ensure victory. One's ability in reasoning

21

or problem solving may be foremost to successfully compete in some structured games. Structured play which emphasizes ability includes games involving most sport activities, electric or board games, cards, and puzzles.

When ability becomes foremost or even a factor in playing, many times the child is placed at a disadvantage to the older person, who has more experience and skill. This difference in ability may fire a competitive spirit within the child to try harder to conquer the opponent, or it may demoralize her to quit because she feels she cannot win or do well.

Challenging children in play to try hard, do their best, and attempt to win is a good incentive, and it teaches children to improve skills to successfully engage in real life. Though this may be a healthy and good emphasis in structured play, the primary emphasis in creative play is far different. Ability is foremost only in the sense of a person's creative use of imagination while playing.

Third Person Imagination

Structured play engages imagination in the third person. Someone else's creativity is active and involved alongside the actual participants. Third person imagination is evident in toys designed to be replicas of the real thing, such as workbenches, refrigerators, stoves, playhouses, model airplanes, and interlocking building blocks.

The child is encouraged to either make believe with another's creative idea or follow the direction built into the toy itself. This type of pretending helps to build a child's confidence in handling those real things in the grown-up's world. The child's imagination is exercised as he pretends with the prefabricated toy. However, another's artistry is still largely responsible for prompting and carrying along the child's make-believing ability.

Structured activity that largely follows the creative pattern or idea of another may reduce the capacity of players to make believe on their own. Again, though, often there is a blend, and the newly finished block truck comes to life, honking and cruising at record speed as the giant driver barely misses the coffee table in the living room.

A Make-Believe Game Is Creative Play

Make-believe games are *emotional* and *physical* vehicles for you to express playful creativity to your child. Besides being fun-filled activities, make-believe games transport vital messages to your child's heart. They effectively communicate your deep desire to establish a loving and lasting relationship with your child.

Emotional Vehicle—The Attitude

Many adults think only in terms of relating with their youngsters in structured play. They play, compete, and challenge their children in a structured game as a means of having fun and as a way of building a better relationship. This is good; however, creative play accomplishes the latter better. Since creative make-believe games are not based on rules, skills, or ability, there is no emotional intimidation to win or do well while playing the game. Rather, the adult and the child are free to design their own comfortably fitted interaction with no other expectation imposed on them.

A structured game that works well for one may not feel comfortable or fit the disposition of the other. The enjoyable common ground of play may be too far apart between the participants. An athletic father trying to play catch with his studious, artistic son may wonder, *How do I get my child interested in playing ball with me?*

Even when the activity fits each individual's personality, the factors of structured play may interfere with the emotional bond developing between the parent and the child. The focus may turn to how well each performs or who wins.

Creative play taps the common interest of children by using colorful make-believe as the basis for an activity. Children naturally love to pretend adventures and events; their interest is easily piqued by imaginative words and expressive body language that suggest a fun exploit is about to begin.

An adult's positive attitude toward creative play helps produce a child's positive emotional response. The adult is using one of the most common elements of childhood, the ability to playfully pretend, as a means of communicating to the child's emotions.

Physical Vehicle—The Activity

Many adults wonder how they are to engage in an imaginative, fun relationship with their children. The wise adult will take cues from the child and attempt to develop imagination by following the child's creativity.

"Come on, Daddy! You do it like this," patiently instructs Susie as she takes a deep breath, dives under the water, and lifts her father's legs apart to make a bridge to swim through. Taking his cue from Susie's attempts to swim between his legs in one breath, the father slowly closes his legs to try to catch his little mermaid. A contest of "I can make it, bet you can't" develops as parent and child engage their creative imagination, each trying to outdo the other in good-natured rivalry. Daddy's mighty bridge may begin to hop up and down as Susie gently tugs at his coarse leg hairs, or Susie may be tickled to the surface as her father nets his little wiggly mermaid.

Creative play offers a tangible way in which the adult and the child can relate well to each other. The attitude and the parent's action are designed to creatively tap into the child's emotions and physical manner of behaving. The make-believe activity gives the adult something creative to do with the child that will capture the child's heart.

The Basic Elements of Creative Play

Positive Use of People or Things

Make-believe games primarily engage a person's imaginative expressions while using people or objects as secondary and as a springboard for the imagination. The use of people or objects is positive. The presence of another person or object fuels the imagination to fuller expression.

Make-believe games use real or imaginary people or objects. Games using real people may involve a child pretending to be Mommy or Daddy or a teacher or a carpenter. Games may include pretending to be something other than a human being, such as a horse, dog, or kitten. Games may involve pretending to be an inanimate object, and the impersonation of the object may be true to real life and accurately follow the way the object performs. For example, the little daughter at the swimming pool tried to swim through her father's legs as if he were a bridge.

Impersonating an object may take a further fantasy direction by the object's coming to life. If the father teasingly moves farther away from his daughter or reaches down to playfully tickle her, he pretends that his leg bridge is moving and acting like a live object might behave.

Positive Competition

There may be a winner and a loser in make-believe games, but being one is just as much fun as being the other in creative play. The fun and intrigue in make-believe games occur by using real or imaginary adventures or challenges.

Make-believe games are to be delightful childlike activities in which you and your child share in constructing an exciting drama through pretend and real events. For instance, a make-believe game using real adventure may be an exploration of the Amazon jungle while you and your child actually hike through a state park. You might use your walking stick to beat a path through the thick vegetation. Birds and squirrels overhead become monkeys chattering at the human intruders searching for the lost temple in the jungle. The activity is staged in a real outdoor setting; however, a make-believe drama also is experienced. Animals, sounds, surroundings—all are imagined as something other than what they are as the game develops.

Or you may explore that same Amazon jungle while walking through your living room. The table, chairs, and couch are dense tropical undergrowth to be crawled around or through to reach the mysteriously hidden jungle temple. The noise of chattering monkeys is imagined as the explorers hear birds chirping outside.

Age and Ability

In creative play, your age is of no importance to how successfully you participate. You are attempting to identify with your child at your child's age level. You may choose to imitate the child's actual chronological age or emotional, maturation level. Matching your child's chronological age means that you behave with more outward childlike actions, words, and behavior. Matching your child's maturation level means that you attempt to identify more on an inner level.

Let's return to the Amazon explorers and see the difference. You may choose to identify with your child as if you are an exuberant young explorer. Your mannerisms, words, and actions take on a childlike quality that closely copy your child's behavior. In effect, you attempt to be a youthful characterization of your child.

You may choose to identify with your child's maturation level while at the same time remaining an adult. You display an emotional and intellectual identity with your child but do not pretend to become a child. You remain the friendly adult companion to the younger, more energetic explorer; however, you emotionally engage your child by remaining in character as the fearless coexplorer on the treacherous jungle expedition. In effect, you attempt to be a mature characterization of your child.

Make-believe games involve age in another way. You and your child may choose to pretend to be totally different ages involving the past or future.

In a make-believe game of the past, the child pretends to be a baby again. The child relives a part of his history, though he may do it with imagined fantasy. He may playfully act out things that never happened to him in real life. In a make-believe game of the future, the child pretends to be a mighty ruler of an island empire.

As with age, ability is irrelevant as far as successfully engaging in make-believe play. There is *no* way to lose as long as each person is participating in a fun and appropriate manner. You and your child are set free to express ideas and imagination without being concerned about playing well or "right" in order to win.

In fact, winning or losing is irrelevant. What *is* relevant is having fun and sharing in a meaningful relationship.

Why Master Make-Believe Games in the First Place?

You should cultivate the creative side of your nature through make-believe activities for three very good reasons. First, you were born creative and expressive. Second, your child longs for creativity in your relationship. Third, vital heart messages are best communicated to your child that way.

1. You Enhance Your God-Breathed Creativity

Why do make-believe games so effectively engage the imagination and allow us to creatively express ourselves? Besides being a real and personal part of an individual, the imagination is God-given. We need only look to the Bible to realize that God-breathed creativity is implanted in everyone. Humans are born creative beings.

Humankind, both male and female, is the wonderful image bearer of God. He declared, "Let Us make man in Our image, according to Our likeness" (Gen. 1:26). God stamps His creative element on the soul of every human as a part of a person's god-likeness. God Himself is intensely creative in His expression and design of our world and of us. Indeed, we are "wonderfully made" (Ps. 139:14). Even if imperfect bearers now, we are creative and expressive image bearers nonetheless.

Adult creativity is implanted, but it needs developing. Make-believe games offer unique ways to tailor creativity along the lines of your personality. Heightening emotional bonding with your child is the purpose of make-believe activities. Learning to use fun creativity to speak to the heart of your child is the art of make-believe.

2. Your Child Longs for a Relationship with You

Make-believe games facilitate your ability to creatively play. When you express your creativity, imagination, and ideas, you significantly interact with your child. Real communication occurs as sharing and understanding take root and grow. Through imaginative games, you share yourself in a fun and adventurous way.

3. Vital Heart Messages Are Communicated

Do you realize all the vital heart messages you normally communicate to your child every day? Make-believe games can increase the number of times you send positive messages in communicating. This, in turn, helps you be more relational in real life on a routine basis.

Make-believe games enable you to send heart messages that speak to your child's inner spirit. In effect, you are conditioning yourself to be more open and accessible to your child through creative play. The result is more positive than negative heart messages.

Sending and Receiving Messages

What are some of these vital heart messages? Chapter 3 looks at three of the most important messages you will ever send to your child. Do you know three of the most important messages you will ever receive from your youngster? Creative play allows the communication to more clearly get through and profoundly affect family members to share a more loving relationship.

Communicate
Vital Heart
Messages

E very parent needs to communicate three vital heart messages to the child. Most children desperately want to communicate three vital heart messages to their parents. What are these messages, and how do make-believe games help in communicating them?

The Parent's Messages

Message #1: "I Value You and Your Childhood"

"Make a wish and blow out the candles, Timmy," coaxes the mother as she finishes lighting the second candle on his beautifully decorated chocolate cake and begins singing "Happy Birthday." In the wonder and excitement of it all, Timmy suddenly reaches out and grabs a handful of cake and stuffs it in his mouth. Turning a chocolate-smeared face to his parents, he laughs with delight as his sticky fingers brush cake crumbs from his mouth. What a mess! Yes. How unexpected! Really? *What do we do now?* wonder the startled parents.

They treasure the moment because the child is precious and they value his childhood. Wise parents will not reprimand, correct, or be truly displeased because celebrating a birthday at age two is a special moment to be experienced and remembered with joy.

Of course, uncontrollably messy behavior is inappropriate. Should Timmy grab a second fistful and begin to fling cake, his parents should quickly intervene and lovingly correct his childish actions. Being tolerant of childlike behavior is quite different from indulging childish misbehavior.

The point of allowing Timmy to take one handful without correction sends this vital heart message: "Yes! Your playful, spontaneous childlike behavior is acceptable because I accept you with all your childhood antics."

The wise parent will view the mess and cleanup as an occasion to strengthen emotional bonds: "Oh, you little rascal! Look at those fingers. They're like muddy chocolate soldiers looking for a bath! Well, finish your piece of cake and lick those fingers clean. Happy birthday, Sweetheart."

Make believing that the child is the commander of the troop of ten sticky mischievous culprits is a gentle reminder to the child to keep order while enjoying the moment. Make-believe games allow the parent to get the point across without becoming inappropriately harsh or exacting. To value a child is to love him and find him precious despite his messes and mistakes. Creative play sends the message loud and clear.

Message #2: "I Know How to Be Childlike, Too"

Look for and engineer as many opportunities as you can to communicate your childlike qualities. Why? All humans, especially the young, desperately long to be affirmed as to who they are. They want to be of value to others, and they wonder whether anyone wants to be like they are.

Why do you think that horsing around, harmless teasing, and mischievous adventures are welcomed with such zeal by children when parents become involved? The big guy being like the little guy communicates a message of acceptance and affirmation to the hearts of the children.

Going back to the birthday cake example, what if each parent follows the child's example and snitches a fingerful of cake? After laughing and enjoying their high-spirited behavior, the mother then neatly cuts three pieces of cake to eat.

This is not to suggest that you should copy every exploit or prank your child invents. But do you copy your child in anything? Do you try to be more youthful and fun like your child? You need to express your inner childlike qualities for the sake of maintaining your emotional health as well as for the sake of sharing in a significant relationship with your youngster. "I want to and can be playfully creative in attitude and actions just like you" is the vital heart message you need to send to your child.

Message #3: "Your Childhood Has a Place in My Adult World"

Every child longs to be the center of someone else's attention. Given the opportunity, most will grab at the chance. Make-believe games help satisfy that desire in a wholesome and acceptable way. When engaging in a creative make-believe game, you are communicating that you will make time for your child and you want to share yourself with her.

"On your mark, get set, go!" challenges the young father as he and his seven-year-old race to spoon lick the mixing bowl clean. Trying to outdo each other for the remaining batter becomes a fun contest in itself, both father and daughter behaving like excited youngsters. For those precious moments, her childhood interests and activities have become his own; her world has found a special time and place in his adult world, and the treasured sense of belonging is communicated between parent and child.

The fact that the father has made a game out of getting the batter allows the child to relate to her father on her level. Most children will race to get the last spoon lick of batter from a mixing bowl. That is the joyful childlike quality of a youngster expressing himself. Granted, almost as quickly, a child will become selfish and grab for his own share and even another's share. The wise parent learns to engage a child on a youthful level and at the same time directs him away from expressing childish (not childlike) behavior.

Learning to invent make-believe games allows you to express your youthfulness in a wholesome and fun way. It allows you to communicate that your youngster's childhood has a special and important place in your adult world.

The Child's Messages

Most youngsters send vital heart messages. Do you know, hear, and receive your child's heart messages daily? Are you facilitating your child's communication to you by your example and interaction?

Message #1: "Be Someone I Want to Be Like When I Grow Up"

Parents are positioned as the first and most significant adult influences in the lives of their children. If circumstances alter this relationship, other adults usually become vital influences. Parents who are present may unknowingly forfeit a life-sustaining and positive impact on their children because they do not relate well to their youngsters. Mastering the skill of creative play through make-believe games helps overcome the generation or personality barriers.

A child deeply desires to have a hero to emulate, an adult to copy. A child sends this vital heart message: "Be my heroes, Mom and Dad!" Most young children instinctively want their parents to be their loving examples to follow.

The thought that your child desperately wants you to be a hero may seem overwhelming. But being creatively playful is an excellent way to become a hero in your child's estimation.

"My dad's the best, most fun guy to be with," proudly exclaims little Johnny to his friends as he shows them the spliced and tied sticks that make up his pretend sword. "We hid behind trees, made believe we fought wild animals, and rescued the princess on our picnic at the lake last Saturday!" Most likely, Johnny will never forget that special time when he and his dad were brave champions in the battle to save the princess. They creatively shared an adventure. The father became a pretend hero in a game and a real hero in his relationship with his son.

Message #2: "Understand My Childhood Like a Good Friend"

Besides wanting them as heroes, children want their parents to be good companions. A child sends this vital heart message: "Mommy and Daddy, be my good friends." Being best friends does not eliminate the adult being a good disciplinarian and leader in the life of a child. Children need wholesome and consistent boundaries of behavior which are set and maintained by a loving adult. Best friends live out their relationship with mutual respect and acceptance. You can learn to build this attitude within your child while creatively playing together.

Try to be a special friend who plays with one of the most precious individuals in your life—your child. Try to understand your child's world as a good friend would. Make-believe games ease your entry into your child's world when feelings of awkwardness may otherwise keep you out.

"Ruth, come here. I'll tell you a secret," invites the mother in a conspiring whisper. Taking her daughter's hand, the mother quickly walks to the couch, sits down, and hides her face behind a throw pillow. Peeking out at the child, she places an index finger on her lips, says, "Shhh," then beckons with her finger for the child to join her behind the pillow.

In this situation, how would a child feel? What would a child think? Whatever creative or playful activity the mother does, she has already gained access into her child's world. She has already communicated her friendship by wanting to share a secret because good friends share secrets and adventures with each other. The wise mother has creatively positioned herself to be perceived by her daughter as such a friend.

"I love you," says the mother and then begins to lightly tickle her daughter under the arms. Joining the fun, the child tickles back. After moments of wrestling, both are out of breath from laughing and end up in a big exhausted bear hug.

Message #3: "Be Someone in Charge of Me, But Be Loving, Too"

Children need to know that they are being looked after and cared for; they need to know that someone somewhere is concerned and cares about them and what happens to them. Many adults feel that consistent, constant oversight might restrict a child's personality and development. Humorless, stringent, or abusive control will. However, being in charge of a child does not mean crushing the child with harsh rules.

The father at the carousel smiles at Lee's squeals of delight as his glossy brown horse flies by again and again. "The ride is over. Time to get off," he calls to his son as the carousel stops. "One more time, please," begs Lee.

The father may do one of several things. He may say no more rides and demand that Lee get off immediately. He may agree to one more ride. Or he may allow himself to be coerced into one of many more rides.

Your child wants someone in authority who lovingly understands and leads. Exercise leadership with tenderness. Attempting to answer yes to wholesome childlike requests will not sacrifice being in charge of your child. The vital heart message of the child is this: "Be in charge of me, but be loving, too."

Unless further delay would really cause a time problem, allowing the child one more ride would probably be the wisest thing to do. The childlike quality of spontaneous joy is being expressed in the child's request. The parent is being given the opportunity to hear the request and to respond with leadership that will encourage that quality rather than crush it.

Allowing children to always have their own way is not creative leadership. Perhaps Lee makes a habit of pushing his wishes to the limit and always tries to get one more ride at the carousel. The wise parent tempers the desire to encourage Lee's spontaneous joy with teaching him respect for authority. The adult exercises his leadership while attempting to connect with the child as a friend would in the relationship.

As a loving parent, try to exercise more humor and generosity as you carry out your leadership responsibilities. Godly authority includes looking out "for the interests of others" (Phil. 2:4) and showing concern for how your child's heart is being affected. The child wants the parent's authority but does not want child-like qualities crushed by it.

True Camaraderie

Togetherness, friendship, and a kindred spirit are powerful influences in a relationship. A sense of true camaraderie must be felt and experienced on a regular basis in order for a relationship to thrive and grow. You need to connect with your child's heart and learn to relate to her while she is young. Cultivating true camaraderie is possible with an older child, but it is more difficult if a firm foundation has not been laid in early childhood.

Becoming a master of make-believe games helps you establish and grow a healthier relationship. It helps you win your child. It allows you to speak from your heart to your child's heart through creative play.

"Gee, Dad! You're fun to be around!" is the likely heart response of a youngster who has just pinned his father on the carpet in a mock wrestling match. Because the parent shares something fun in common with his child, the child more readily identifies the parent as a friend. Creative play focuses more on the relationship being developed than on the activity being performed (as in structured play).

Make-believe games increase the child's receptivity to parental leadership and authority. The adult has the opportunity to share leadership and authority in a pleasurable activity.

"Dad, get down now!" excitedly instructs seven-year-old Mark as he and his father duck behind the closet door and try to elude the female search party in the game of hide-and-seek. The young son is telling the father what to do. The child command-ing the adult is acceptable because both are equals playing in a game. The adult's willingness to share leadership and even submit to the child's instruction sends a clear message that goodwill and true camaraderie exist in their relationship.

Seek to arrange as many occasions as possible where this will occur. Experiencing shared command and leadership in a make-believe game reduces your child's longing to be, for once, in charge of a situation and win over or direct you. Such a conces-sion to a child in real life can be very harmful and destructive if allowed often. However, in a make-believe game, it is all part of the fun.

In make-believe games, true camaraderie is conveyed by you to your child and by your child to you. Your child observes first-hand your sincere attempt and effort to emulate or copy child-like youthfulness. And your youngster is in the unique position of teaching you the tips of the trade in being creatively playful. Granting welcomed inclusion into the world of creative play is one of the deepest expressions of true friendship and cama-raderie your child can give to you. It is also one that most chil-dren gladly give if asked.

Make-believe games give the imaginative touch to creative play. They secure your child's heart in a wholesome bond to yours. Your effort, skill, and ability to creatively play contribute to winning the treasure of a more loving and close relationship with your child.

Sending and receiving heart messages reveal your deep de-sires to meaningfully interact with family members. The manner in which you communicate the messages is vital. You need to understand and capture the spirit behind creative play so that you can send heart messages to your child. Chapter 4 reveals the profound dynamics of the spirit of creative play.

CHAPTER 2

Catch the Spirit
of Creative Play

"The big, bad wolf came up to the second little piggy's house of sticks," reads Dad while Ruth nestles against her father, anticipating the excitement of the story time adventure.

"Little pig! Little pig! Let me come in!" says Dad in his deep voice, pretending to be the wolf growling out his threat.

Then as the little pig, Dad alters his voice to a high-pitched squeal and taunts back, "Not by the hair of my chinny chin chin!"

Again as the wolf, Dad snarls in his deepest voice, "Then I'll huff and I'll puff and I'll blowww your house in!" And shaking Ruth as if great gusts of wind are whirling past, he and his daughter tumble off the living room chair, laughing together on the carpet.

What is original? Just a beloved story creatively read and put into action by an interested parent. Anyone can do it. That is exactly the point. If anyone can, why don't more parents do it?

Creative play is a natural means of expression—only adults have forgotten how to communicate in this language form. Why is it difficult for adults to release themselves to spontaneous behavior like make-believe or romping playfulness with a child? Let's look at four basic reasons.

Four Adult Types Who Find Creative Play Difficult

The first type of adult does not know how to recapture a creatively playful spirit and feels discouraged by awkward attempts to do so. This willing, but inhibited, adult truly desires to creatively play but hesitates because of inexperience. This grown-up is teachable and will most easily capture the spirit behind imaginative expression. Given the opportunity, that little child residing within will surface, rediscovering the long forgotten, yet vaguely familiar ways of communicating in the language of creative play.

The second type of adult believes that childlike behavior is equivalent to childish behavior. Therefore, it is inappropriate and foolish for grown-ups to engage in creative play that is childlike in nature. This unwilling and inhibited adult may be won if shown the vast difference between wholesome imaginative play and unhealthy silliness. This adult possesses youthful creativity that is healthy to express.

The third type of adult fails to comprehend the power of creative play in building a relationship between adult and child. This uninformed adult feels overwhelmed and exhausted by the endless demands of raising children and simply does not want to shoulder another responsibility, especially a seemingly unnecessary one. Experiencing the profound dynamics of friendship and unity that occur in creative play will convince the adult of its importance in a relationship.

The fourth type of adult has a disposition and a personality not naturally inclined to being playfully creative. This adult's comfort zone seldom stretches beyond an occasional relaxing of a dignified response. However, profoundly touching a child's heart is well worth a little relational discomfort and initial awkwardness. The enclosed adult can stretch narrow playfulness by focusing on what is most beneficial to the child rather than what is most comfortable personally. The laughter, delight, and endearment of a child creatively engaged in wholesome fun are great incentives to encourage an enclosed adult to be more youthfully expressive.

The Kindred Spirit

Catching the spirit behind creative play is necessary to successfully engage in communicating in this language form. Ask yourself, What kind of parent does my child perceive me to be? Can he snuggle up closely, or must he approach cautiously at a distance? Does she sense her presence is a welcomed inclusion or an annoyance to be tolerated? Do you belly laugh over endearing foibles of childhood, or are your reactions characterized by a humorless parental response?

In your child's estimation, are you warm or cold, near or far, in your parental relationship with him? Granted, your and your child's emotional makeup and expression may register over a wide range of responses given each individual's unique personality, physical health, and past or present circumstances.

Does your child sense a kindred spirit toward you? In your relationship as parent and child, is there a resounding ring in his heart that you and he are made up of the same stuff, that in very special ways, you are best buddies?

What is the kindred spirit so essential for you to catch and express that is behind successfully engaging in creative play? The kindred spirit is the felt sense that endearing and profound alikeness exists and is communicated between individuals. It is your child's heart awareness that in certain ways and at certain times, you think, feel, and act similarly to her and you truly understand her.

You may consciously and even unconsciously convey a kindred spirit to your child at times. However, occasionally seizing the moment to express oneness with your child will inadequately fill your child's vast reservoir of emotional and psychological need to be significantly identified with you. It is far better to take advantage of spontaneous, natural moments and to masterfully create moments of communicating a kindred spirit. So, what are the components of a kindred spirit?

Element #1 of the Kindred Spirit:
We're Made of the Same Stuff

One of the deepest longings of a child is to know that he belongs, is akin, to another. Even adults desire to satisfy this deep human hunger to be significantly identified, connected, or attached to another, even if only through the past. Many adults desperately try to find their roots and discover from where they have come and to whom they belong. Though not everyone is able to identify or uncover biological family connections, most people are capable of experiencing a psychological or emotional oneness with another.

A child needs to feel that she and her parent are made of the same stuff if heartfelt communication is to occur. A child doesn't relate well to a parent who is perceived as a distant, cold authority figure.

Being made of the same stuff is more than a biological connection with another. It may be strongly felt between people who are totally unrelated by birth or heredity. It is a felt oneness in spirit with another. It is feeling that we—you and me—are alike. We are made out of something profoundly, wonderfully the same. For a parent and a child, does the flavor of alikeness exist anywhere in the relationship?

"You little rascal, you're as scampish as a squirrel collecting nuts!" declares the mother as she and her four-year-old make a game of scurrying to pick up twigs for the campfire. The parent is not just gathering wood to get the fire started. She is encouraging the natural motion and enthusiasm of her young child in a playful manner while doing a work activity. The child unconsciously reasons, *She must like picking up sticks as much as I do,* and he makes an emotional notch in his little mind of just one more way they are alike.

Take advantage of the ways you are naturally similar to your child in attitudes and actions, and playfully construct ways to be similar. How do you learn to communicate to your child that both of you are made of the same stuff (or at least you want to be made of the same stuff as your child)?

Remember and Relive

Remember your childhood. Let out that little child concealed within your grown-up exterior.

Remember when the tall tree in the backyard with its low hanging branches called you to be an adventurous mountain climber? Or the mud puddles down your street were little lakes you stomped through as the great giant after the rain? Remember the brown cardboard box that became your boat, wildly riding the ocean waves? Or the hidden cave constructed with sheets behind the sofa in the family room?

Most adults can recall from memory treasured childhood experiences that are wholesome and positive. You smile as you see yourself again as the sticky-faced youngster licking a dripping cone of your favorite ice cream. Isn't ice cream fun to play with and taste on your tongue? Whether a child making a pleasurable mess or an adult neatly eating it, isn't the experience delightful? It's not so different whether you are an adult or a child when it comes to enjoying ice cream.

You will discover just how much you and your child are made of the same stuff *if* you will release the little child within and share a present experience with remembered, relived child-like enjoyment. Of course, you won't smear your face with ice cream so that you can experience along with your four-year-old the abandonment of a child licking a dripping cone! But child-hood joys are a means of identifying with your child and com-municating that you enjoy the same things.

"This is sooo good, and you're a real little mess!" playfully chides the father as he takes a big lick of ice cream off his own cone and gently wipes the messy fingers and smiling face of his youngster.

"You and I are made of the same stuff" is further communi-cated when the child sees the father's unsuccessful efforts to lick all the drips off his own cone and even spills a chunk of ice cream when he takes a bite. *Gee, Dad, you're kind of messy, too!* mentally observes the child, even voicing his opinion in a joking way.

If the dad is a little playful with the accident, a greater kin-dred spirit is communicated. Why? We're really made of the same stuff when it comes to the sticky business of eating a drip-ping ice-cream cone. The adult and the child are alike in the same experience. If both laugh together over their messy acci-dents, the kindred spirit is more fully realized. In effect, the adult is saying to the child, "I'm like you. You're like me. I like being like you." The vital heart messages of love, friendship, and acceptance are conveyed to the child's receptive heart as he shares this experience with his parent.

Element #2 of the Kindred Spirit:
We're Good Friends

"Get these clothes picked up right now!" angrily demands the mother who walks back to her son's bedroom to kiss him good night and discovers his wet Little League uniform crumpled on the floor again.

Although children should be disciplined for continual or repeated disobedience, do not forget the sympathy and understanding that good friends show each other. Friends make allowances, give the benefit of the doubt, and at times choose to overlook a matter rather than take issue.

Balance consistent discipline with understanding of a child's makeup, and occasionlly respond as a friend: "OK! Big Guy, you're tired and falling asleep. I'll capture these bandit clothes and throw them in the wash this time. Good night, Sweetheart. Great game!" Responding as a good friend lending aid to an exhausted buddy expresses the kindred spirit. Such demonstrations of friendship will deeply touch a child's heart because the grown-up authority figure knows how to be a caring companion, a best buddy.

Basic Attitudes Shared by Good Friends

What are basic attitudes shared by good friends? They take turns leading and following each other. This give-and-take attitude allows more balanced and equal interaction. There is not a top dog mentality that makes a little tyrant out of a would-be playmate. Nor is there an underdog mentality that subjects a child to a constant second-place position in the relationship.

Esteem is another vital ingredient shared between good friends. This you-first-and-me-last attitude minimizes selfish exalting or demeaning of each other. A good friend "esteem[s] others better than himself . . . [and looks out] for the interests of others" (Phil. 2:3–4). This attitude is reflected when Tommy offers Jimmy the first lick of his lollipop or when Susan holds a hidden treat in each hand, allowing Anne first pick.

Good friends communicate well with each other. This talk-and-listen attitude allows healthy verbal interaction. One may do more talking and the other more listening, but it is by mutual agreement and consent, not by forced one-sided domination; it is a natural outworking of friends learning to like, accept, and read each other.

Good friends like and feel comfortable with each other. This I-can-be-me-with-you attitude relaxes the relationship. Good friends feel the liberty to strongly express opinions and differences but not in an overly hostile manner. Tim's "No, you can't!" counters Johnny's "Yes, I will!" and though the two may argue and even separate for the afternoon, they meet again as good friends to play in the backyard the next day.

Observe how these qualities of a good friend are demonstrated in the ice-cream episode. The father encourages the child as his best buddy and captures the youngster's heart more securely.

Best Buddies Eating Ice Cream Together

The father and the child experience the joy of eating a messy ice-cream cone. The give-and-take attitude is shared when the dad playfully cleans up his son's sticky fingers and the son watches the father struggle to lick all the drips on his own cone. Both equally enjoy the ice-cream cone experience as friends; they share the adventure; they laugh about and enjoy the ups and downs.

The you-first-and-me-last attitude is illustrated by the very fact that the father takes time out of his busy schedule to eat an ice-cream cone with his youngster. The adult places his relationship with the child above his personal agenda and makes it a priority.

The talk-and-listen attitude is revealed when the father allows his son to comment on and laugh about the mess the father makes while eating his ice cream. Each has something to say about the other, and each listens to the other's response. There is a sense of mutual acceptance and regard.

The child is encouraged to have the I-can-be-me-with-you attitude because the father does not criticize or scold but playfully enjoys to some extent the child's messy mishaps. The father allows himself to be relaxed and forgo polished table manners.

The kindred spirit of good friends is experienced when parent and child treat each other as mutual companions in certain experiences and at certain times. You should not feel obligated to always relate to your child as a companion; it is a privilege to be experienced on occasion. Construct as many appropriate occasions as possible so your child experiences being a best buddy to the most significant adult in his life—you.

Element #3 of the Kindred Spirit: Right Now, We're Equals

You need to correctly grasp this important, but tricky, concept to communicate the kindred spirit to your child. Being equal with your youngster in creative play does not mean that you cease being an authoritative role model to your child in real life.

An aggressive five-year-old allowed equal standing with the parent will rapidly become licensed in her behavior. She will take liberties and become disrespectful, disobedient, and abusive. She will view the adult as a comrade who is not really in charge.

The idea of being equals refers to a psychological equality in which you pretend to be on the same age level as your child in a playful activity. Both of you know this is just a part of the game; you are not really giving up parental authority.

As mentioned earlier, you may pretend to be either the chronological age or the psychological age of your child. The former would sound something like this: "My turn to hide and you go seek!" playfully insists the young dad as he ducks behind the closet door and calls out for his four-year-old to begin counting. The father physically and emotionally behaves like an energetic youngster. The latter would sound something like this: "Two cups of sand sugar and a half-cup of dirt should make it real tasty," thoughtfully states the mother as she helps her four-year-old stir in the final ingredients for mud pies. The mother maintains her adult composure but psychologically engages in a child's make-believe game of cooking.

Communicating equality means that you do not talk down to your child. Baby talk—unless to a baby—is an inappropriate form of relating. You should attempt to come alongside your youngster. Identifying with your child means engaging him intelligently and creatively with childlike energy and interest.

Likewise, you should discourage your youngster from acting too grown-up or too old for her age. Your child may attempt to identify with you by becoming more mature in her actions. This does not include playing dress up or house with your things. Healthy identification with the grown-up world is good as it prepares a child for maturity. For example, a seven-year-old who wants to regularly wear makeup is acting too old for her age. She is taking too seriously a make-believe activity. A good rule of thumb is to help your child keep and enjoy childhood as long as possible.

The Capturing Spirit

There is a second major factor to catching the spirit of playful creativity. To win your child's heart, you must learn the skill of communicating a capturing spirit. The kindred spirit deals with your child's inner, emotional identification with you. The capturing spirit deals with how you carry on playful creativity, how you enable your child to more easily identify with you.

Learning to have a capturing spirit helps you increase the times of positive relational interaction with your child. Creating excitement and adventure out of everyday activities of home life profoundly affects a child. It encourages your child to want to lovingly relate to you.

Learning to be creatively playful can be like stepping into a canoe. At first you feel a little unsure of your footing, a little afraid of losing your balance and tipping. Remembering the three basic elements of the capturing spirit will help you stay balanced and make creative play a wonderful experience for you and your child.

Making It Fun

"Quick! Roger, get the box of oatmeal and put it in the truck before we take off!" instructs the mother who is grocery shopping down the cereal aisle. Sitting in the front of the cart is her toddler, and walking on either side of the basket are her five-year-old son and seven-year-old daughter.

Truck in the cereal aisle? What is going on here? Who would have ever thought of that? Your child would have if allowed to express imagination.

A child knows how to creatively make fun out of the ordinary. Why do you think the plate of spaghetti draws the attention of the toddler? It is fun to feel and taste the noodles. Of course, the child should be taught polite table manners; however, the parent should be just as eager to capture the child's spirit in the process. "Oh! Look at this shiny pile of food! Let's pretend you're a big human crane and scoop it up neatly with your fork," says the mother as she gently holds the fork in her toddler's hand and helps him carefully finish his meal.

Learning to express fun in an activity is the first element of a capturing spirit. The fun should be a natural outworking of the routine activity. Think of it this way. To a child, a big shopping cart looks every bit like a vehicle, especially if the child sits in the basket. Take it a step further. If older children are instructed to hold on to the sides and walk while the mother pushes the cart, the vehicle looks very much like a big truck, into which they load all kinds of supplies.

The parent expresses a capturing spirit when she consciously turns what could be a rather dull experience of shopping for food into an occasion for having fun. She captures their interest by suggesting they help collect items and put them in the truck to take back home. That is, the children get the food off the shelves and put it in the shopping basket as the mother pushes the cart down the aisles.

A child's age is a big consideration when capturing interest. Asking a three-year-old to pick up a mayonnaise jar to put in the cart could be more disastrous than fun. Structuring the action to fit the child's age and ability ensures a happy conclusion to making fun out of the ordinary.

Catching Interest

The second element of a capturing spirit is catching your child's creative interest. Most children will readily respond to being playfully creative if it is not forced on them.

Creative play is not something your child *has* to do. You invite her to join you. As with any invitation, it may be accepted or rejected. Do not demand that your child accept. Do not subject your child to feelings of guilt for turning down the invitation. Such attitudes or actions definitely will not communicate a capturing spirit.

"Susan, there's the detergent on the lower shelf up ahead! Let's collect it at our next stop," points out the mother to her seven-year-old daughter. For whatever reason, Susan may be less enthusiastic about pretending to gather supplies than her five-year-old brother. Therefore, the child should not be forced to retrieve the soap box if she expresses feelings of hesitation, embarrassment, or discomfort.

Welcomed inclusion rather than forced participation is crucial on the parent's part. If Susan flatly refuses to pick up the detergent, the mother quickly assigns that privilege and duty to the younger brother. This should be done not in a commanding, demeaning manner but in a light, playful manner. The adult is eagerly looking for some special boy or girl with whom to play the pretend game. "Do join us if you want. It's OK if you don't" is to be the attitude conveyed to the children.

To improve the chances for your child to willingly accept your invitation to creatively play, stay in character. Stay in character even if the child declines to play. Remember, it is wholesome, healthy, and good for you to express playful creativity whether or not your child joins you in the fun.

Should Susan's younger brother hesitate to get the detergent, the mother should conclude the food collection on a happy note. She might say, "Well, team, great job! Everything is almost picked up. I guess we've about finished."

Perhaps the enjoyment of the game is over, or the children are getting tired. There are any number of legitimate reasons to stop. In creative play, a child's refusal should not be regarded as disobedient behavior as it would be in real life. Good friends who are equals have freedom to say yes and no to each other in play.

Finally, the capturing spirit of creative play will be communicated to and caught by your child if you remain friendly and good-humored. A faultfinding attitude does great damage to the heart and spirit of a child. *There must be something wrong with me,* reasons the child.

A child's inappropriate conduct and behavior should be corrected. However, being harmfully judgmental or critical will crush the spirit whereas "pleasant words are like a honeycomb, sweetness to the soul and health to the bones" (Prov. 16:24). In creative play as in real life, you should instruct, nurture, and guide your child, not discourage her by harsh criticism.

A parent may become frustrated and overly critical when his good intentions on behalf of the child are ignored or rejected. A well-meaning father might say with hurt exasperation, "Why can't you ever join in? Why can't you ever be a part of this family?" The father's ten-year-old son has just refused to wrestle with him and a younger brother in a playful bout of king of the mountain.

When a parent's positive sentiment is attached to a why-can't-you criticism, there is a negative impact on the relationship. Though the father really wants his son to participate in a wholesome, loving manner, the son hears only the critical rebuke and closes his heart more tightly against the relationship.

Communicating a capturing spirit will attempt to win the child's heart. "Hey, help me when you want! This tough wrestler is wearing me out! I need you, Big Guy! Please, please help me!" playfully implores the father. Coaxing a child in a gentle, kind, and loving manner will do far more to connect with his heart than demanding his participation.

Being Imaginative

As for the third element, the capturing spirit communicates an imaginative interest and attempts to fan rather than subdue creative expression. Learning to be imaginative takes practice.

First, you need to recognize that these special occasions are the delightful moments of childhood of which memories are made. These times are to be treasured, visually implanted in the mind, emotionally engraved on the heart, and physically experienced together with your child.

Being imaginative is more than telling a child to *go* and *do* something away from you. It is inviting a child to *come* and *share* something with you. "Oh! You'll look just like Daddy! Please, come and show me after you get all dressed up!" is how a mother can express her interest to her child when he requests permission to borrow Daddy's old suit.."Here's an old tie, too!" is how she can add her creative touch to the adventure.

Second, you need to understand yourself and your style of relating. It is futile and frustrating to attempt to act in ways contrary to your basic makeup. A naturally reserved adult should not attempt to become animated. A talkative adult should not attempt to become subdued.

Third, you need to be an active participant rather than a passive spectator in a child's world of play. Many adults suppose that observing their children's activities with a benevolent attitude or at a distance is sufficient to count for participation in childhood creativity. It is not.

To communicate a capturing spirit, you must be truly imaginative and be an active participant in the playful event. You add your creative touch rather than just stand by and admire the experience. You express your imagination and artistry and make a profound impression on your child's heart.

The creative mother will set aside for a moment the vacuuming of the living room, walk out to the backyard with a plateful of cookies, and pretend to be a door-to-door saleswoman: "Hello, Mr. Jones. Would you like to buy these delicious cookies for your lovely family? They're on sale today for only three rocks and two leaves."

The parent participates in the child's world with the capturing spirit of her imagination. This activity is a wholesome reprieve from her adult world of responsibilities, and she communicates the love and identity she longs to share with her child.

Touching the Heartstrings

The kindred, capturing spirit is the attitude behind creative play. It allows you to identify with your child as good friends sharing a fun-filled activity. The gentle and loving way in which you communicate this is very important. Chapter 5 discusses the three touches on the heartstrings of a child.

Three Touches of the Kindred, Capturing Spirit

To express the kindred, capturing spirit of creative play, you need to be aware of three important touches: the touch of innocence, the touch of gentleness, and the touch of laughter.

The Touch of Innocence

In creative play, you must always guard against anything wicked being introduced into the relationship. The world offers no reliable basis for determining what is wicked. But the Scriptures make very clear what is meant by evil attitudes, words, and actions. Romans 1:18–31 points out that wickedness is turning away from the Christlike conduct that God commands of created human beings.

The touch of innocence means that goodness is honored and wickedness is not. However, even apart from biblical teaching, the inner consciousness of right and wrong is engraved on the human heart by God and helps to morally guide a person in what is honorable (Rom. 2:5–16).

The three categories of wrong behavior to avoid in creative play are unkind conduct, cruel conduct, and perverse conduct.

Unkind Conduct

The first and most common category of wrong behavior is unkind conduct: attitudes, words, or actions that could be labeled as hurtful. It may be sarcastic little comments that hurt the feelings of another or physical or overly rowdy actions that cause discomfort or pain to a child.

Many times this conduct is unintentional. A comment is quickly spoken without any real thought of damaging the heart or spirit of the child. "Jeff! What do you think you're doing? Put all your pillows and sheets back on your bed and untie that ridiculous rope from around the chair. Now!" commands the mother when she discovers her son's makeshift fort in the enemy territory of his bedroom.

Or the action is intended to be fun, but the adult forgets to be careful. "Oh, don't be such a big crybaby, Stevie! Be a man when you wrestle with me!" taunts the father whose quick turn caused his little son to fall backward and hit his elbow.

These words and actions may not sound wrong. They are impatient comments or accidents in the normal activities of family life. Probably such responses do not come from any deep-seated or wicked hostility on the part of the parent. However, such responses communicate a hurtful message to the heart of the child: "I don't care about your pain or whether you're disappointed."

In creative play, to be insensitive or unkind or to inflict pain, whether accidentally or purposefully, is destructive to a

relationship. It is more the absence of the caring touch of innocence than the presence of real evil that makes such responses
wrong and so destructive to a relationship.

For creative play to communicate a kindred, capturing spirit,
the child must feel the touch of innocence. That you want to be
caring and gentle to your child in word or action must be the
message she receives in her heart. You must be willing to admit
and apologize for hurtful conduct when it occurs.

Cruel Conduct

The second major category of wrong behavior is cruel words
and conduct. Such activity could be classified as hateful.

The parent angrily yells, "Look at this mess, you stupid idiot!
What do you think you're doing?" She yanks her daughter out
of the half-emptied bathtub. Throwing towels on the floor to
mop up the sudsy water, the mother impulsively slaps her little
girl's behind and commands her never to pretend to be a splashing mermaid in the bathtub again.

A caring adult who wants to communicate the kindred,
capturing spirit in a relationship must control cruel outbursts
in words and actions. A child needs to be guided and corrected
for misbehavior, but humiliating, demeaning, or harsh correction is a cruel mishandling of parental authority. That's especially
true if the child was not really conscious of the mess she was
making.

"Emily, look at this mess! If you're going to play mermaid,
keep the water in the tub, Honey! Get out of there. You need
to help me mop up the water with these towels." The parent
who corrects a child in this way will more successfully win
the child's heart than the parent whose response is harsh and
cruel.

Perverse Conduct

The third broad category of wrong behavior is perverse conduct: words or actions that are immodest or immoral in nature. Most adults recognize perversion in its more blatant expressions and attempt to steer their children away from it. However, far less are aware of its beginnings. Playful creativity never is immodest or indiscreet. Any real, suggested, or imagined action that would move an activity in an immodest direction is perverse and not creative playfulness.

The adult defuses the child's natural curiosity about sexuality by making a playfully creative and nonthreatening activity out of the normal events surrounding a child of the opposite sex. For instance, a mother diapering the baby could engage an older brother's help: "We've got to flour the bottom of this little biscuit so she won't get all sticky. Would you get the talcum powder, Luke?"

Allowing children to participate in natural family duties rather than making things forbidden is a good way to reduce their curiosity. It also lessens the tendency of children to engage in secretive directions. Creative play encourages children's wholesome and inquisitive exploration but not immodest investigation of others and the world around them.

The Touch of Gentleness

The touch of gentleness refers to how the adult actually handles the child. Being too rough generally occurs when the grown-up forgets himself in the spirit of the game. He unintentionally handles his child with excessive rowdiness. "Daddy! Let go! That hurts!" cries Jeff as the father playfully grabs his young son's wrist to make him drop the squirt gun and surrender his weapon.

Most definitely, there should not be actual hostility between the parent and the child when they creatively play. Truly combative attitudes, words, and actions are totally inappropriate. "Gotcha! Now you're it!" smirks the impatient father as he lands a hard slap rather than a light tag on the bottom of his energetic and insistent three-year-old. Often the parent and the child attempt to settle the score by hurtful underhanded play.

Masking negative feelings in an abusive playful context is not only hypocritical and deceitful, but it usually does not work. Why will a child laughingly engage in really physical roughhousing in play but cry at a token painless swat in correction? Physical romping, even when it borders on being too rough, is tolerated, often welcomed, by a young child when no real hurtful or corrective handling is intended by the adult. Likewise, when a child senses true adult displeasure or ill will, even a light swat, pull, or touch may bring that child to tears. Creative play is not to be used in any way to hurtfully get back at or correct a child over some unresolved problem.

Expressing the touch of gentleness means that you are keenly aware of how to begin and end a playful activity. Beginning play may be sudden, but you should not abruptly end the activity.

The adult may spontaneously begin a game. "Now you're it!" says the relaxed father as he suddenly jumps up from his chair, playfully touches his young son, and darts out of the family room. Instantly, a game of chase ensues with the child hot on the heels of his father.

You should gently end a playful activity unless circumstances make a quick conclusion unavoidable. Avoid being perceived as a killjoy to fun if at all possible.

"This little piggy went to market. This little piggy stayed home. This little piggy ate roast beef. This little piggy had none.

And this little piggy went wee, wee, wee all the way home." The young father croons the beloved nursery rhyme as he wiggles and tickles the toddler's chubby little toes. After several rounds, the father must return to the business of putting on his youngster's shoes and socks.

"OK, Dana. One last time and then we have to put your cute toes into your socks and tennis shoes." The father gently prepares his child for ending the play; he alerts his daughter that the game will soon be over.

The touch of gentleness attempts to bring the child smoothly rather than abruptly back into the real world. Gently ending creative play allows the child to more easily come down from the laughter and excitement of happily interacting with you. If you too quickly cut off imaginative expression, the child may view you as a big person who doesn't know how to play right. You can unwittingly damage good communication and alienate a young child's heart if you end fun too quickly, especially fun that you introduce and begin.

The touch of gentleness applies to the child, too. Guide your child away from practicing inappropriate behavior that is hurtful, out of control, or disrespectful. You condone and encourage rude and rowdy conduct when you allow its unbridled expression. Your child should never be allowed to use discourteous or derogatory terms in jest. This is verbal abuse, not creative play. "Daddy's a big fat pig! Daddy's a big fat pig!" squeals the five-year-old daughter trying to escape capture by her father in a game of tag.

Be sensitive, and do not humiliate or dampen your child's spirit by an angry correction. A gentle reminder to an excited and energetic child should sound friendly and give an alternative response: "Mary, I love to play tag with you, but it's not polite to call people names, even when we're playing. You can say, 'Daddy can't get me!'"

Your child should not be allowed to physically abuse you in creative play. Painfully striking, yanking, biting, or scratching is inappropriate. But don't confuse physically abusive action with a token swat, tug, or pull that may occur in creative activity.

In creative play, the adult on all fours pretends to be a romping horse. The child pretends to handle the adult as if he is a horse—patting him gently on the head, giving a playful swat to the rear end, bouncing up and down on his back to get him moving. For the child to forcefully strike the adult with the hand or heel, as one might do to a real horse, is inappropriate roughness. Creative play is not physically or verbally abusive. It communicates the touch of gentleness in attitude, words, and actions.

The Touch of Laughter

The touch of laughter is merriment that goes beyond the actual laughter and pleasant exchange between parent and child. Communicating delight through laughter means that the adult playfully expresses endearment that singles out the child as uniquely special. Constructing this type of fun-filled event conveys the parent's love, friendship, and acceptance of the child.

The touch of laughter is a subtle but powerful form of expression that promotes real emotional bonding between parent and child. Properly balancing the three elements of the touch of laughter profoundly communicates a kindred, capturing spirit to the child's heart.

Teasing That Is Good

"You're my favorite blonde-haired, blue-eyed five-year-old girl!" proudly declares the mother of seven to her youngest daughter. She may even say this in the presence of her other children. "How awful! How cruel!" you respond, and you would be correct—except for one fact. The youngest daughter is the only blonde-haired, blue-eyed five-year-old girl in the family. This obvious fact does not escape the notice of her daughter or the other children, so playful delight rather than hurtful favoritism is communicated.

The mother may take this creative game a step farther. On purpose, she singles out each child as uniquely special by admiring some exclusive quality or trait. In effect, the mother of seven creatively expresses her delight with each child without inciting sibling rivalry.

Where does the touch of laughter come into effect? The mother gives her compliment with parental authority. She is serious and sincere, yet there is a slight twinkle in her eye, a little curve of a smile at the corners of her mouth, a playful intonation to her voice. The children distinctively know that a parent should not openly show favoritism. But their mother is doing just that and seemingly enjoying it. "There must be a catch. Is this a joke? She's teasing us! Deb is the only blonde, blue-eyed girl in our family!" they finally reason.

The adult must give the endearing comment in honest sincerity. However, it is the delightful twist that is enjoyed and laughed about. Why does this type of verbal interchange so powerfully touch a child's heart? Children tease! That is a natural characteristic of youngsters—usually one that is hurtful or destructive to relationships. The parent is effectively communicating in their language by using a negative characteristic in a creative, positive manner. The mother's teasing is blended with the positive quality of childlike sincerity and not the negative quality of childish comparison.

The adult may even add a boastful quality to her teasing. Why? Children boast! That is also a natural characteristic of youngsters—usually one that adults try to discourage. Again, the mother is taking a natural quality and constructively using it to communicate in a youngster's language rather than speaking destructively. Her boastful comment might sound something like this: "In fact, if you lined up all the blonde-haired, blue-eyed five-year-old girls in the whole world, I'd pick you! You're my favorite!"

The mother is not only bragging; she is pretending to be very select when there is no real competition. All her children know that her boastful bragging is just a teasing and delightful expression of her sincere love for the child. The child cannot help winning the contest because no other child fits the requirements the mother has established.

How can a parent master this skill? How can she keep from getting mixed up in expressing good and bad teasing? Good teasing is fundamentally based on communicating wholesome goodwill and delight to the child. The child receives this vital heart message: "Mama is pleased with me and who I am." The parent is purposefully showing her favor, endearment, and regard for her child, yet she is doing it in a fun-filled way. Bad teasing shows real partiality that pits one child against another. That is extremely destructive to a family and is totally opposite to the spirit of playful creativity.

A parent's love and acceptance may be expressed without adding the touch of laughter. The mother may express her affection in a more customarily parental manner: "Deb, you're my precious littlest girl, and I love you dearly." When a parent's endearment is sincerely communicated, a powerful message of acceptance and well-being is sent to the child.

Expressing your love with a creative touch of laughter helps the message of love get through to the heart of your child. Skillfully mastering the ability to tease with wholesome goodwill is one of the surest marks that you are communicating a kindred, capturing spirit. A child is usually game for fun. If playful mystery is added to the enjoyment, you are almost assured of gaining your child's attention, interest, and allegiance in the relationship.

A second element of the touch of laughter captures the heart of a child. It is practicing playful mischievousness.

Mischievousness That Is Good

Two-year-old Jimmy gets completely entangled as he uncoils the entire roll of toilet paper in the bathroom. Observe the shiny grin of delight on his face at his great accomplishment. Think how he might lift his chubby arms to be picked up for a hug. In spite of the mess, the sight may be cute, too.

Children are naturally inquisitive and oftentimes mischievous in their exploration of the world. Parents should not make light of or ignore willful disobedience, but many parents make too heavy a case against their young children. Parents who do not recognize with delight children's youthful, inquisitive, and mischievous nature will find it hard to laugh with enjoyment over the wonderful world called growing up.

These parents need to lighten up. They need to recognize those frazzled, yet precious, moments when they come unexpectedly. They need to respond with a measure of endearment toward the children rather than with harsh or humorless correction.

Even when the child gets entangled in mischief, the parent needs to wisely show affirmation and acceptance of the good inquisitive aspect of the child's nature. By affirming, the adult recognizes childish mishaps for what they so often are—innocent, immature mistakes or inabilities of the child. By acceptance, the adult still finds the youngster lovable and endearing, perhaps even more so because of the youthful antics.

Beyond learning a measure of benevolent toleration and enjoyment toward some of the natural mishaps of a youngster, the parent who learns to engage in wholesome and good mischievousness with the child will speak to the very heart of the child. Why? Children are born mischief makers, and the adult who creatively joins in an exploit will win the child over to a more loving relationship.

This is not to suggest that the adult introduces or endorses anything really bad, hurtful, or unkind. Rather, the adult plots innocent, harmless mischief, and then the grown-up tries to encourage and persuade the child to follow. In effect, the adult becomes the ringleader of mischief instead of the officer who squelches a little rascally fun.

"Tonight, just for fun, we're having dessert first!" announces the mother to her young family, and the children gleefully giggle at their mother's naughty behavior. Oh, the delight of eating a small piece of cake before eating meat and potatoes. The mother may add a teasing note to the fun: "Now, no complaining or arguing about it! It won't do you any good. You *have* to eat every last bite of your cake before you get any green beans!"

A child should not be pampered and accommodated every time something runs counter to her desires and wishes. Learning to submit her will to the authority and direction of another is an invaluable lesson in life, which every child needs to experience. However, the parent needs to learn how to winsomely meet needs and try to satisfy some of the child's secret longings, even the mischievous ones.

Good mischief is by definition *good*. Having a small piece of chocolate cake before dinner may spoil the child's appetite for one meal, but it certainly will not damage him physically. Should the youngster refuse to eat his supper the next night unless he gets cake first, the wise parent will not pamper the child's willfull attempt to be in charge. Rather, the loving and authoritative parent will explain that mischievous adventures are fun breaks from routines; they are creative exceptions to the normal way of doing things; they are special times to be remembered, enjoyed, and looked forward to occasionally.

Good mischief causes your child to perceive you as a companion who knows how to share in secret desires and dreams. *You really understand me after all*, reasons the child after he watches his mother enjoying, every bit as much as he does, the delicious cake before dinner. She may get a fingerful of icing from the cake before cutting the slices and—wonder of wonders—invite her children to do the same thing!

The mischievous touch of laughter allows you to wholesomely include yourself in your child's world of adventure, longings, and discovery and to make a special difference by being there. This leads directly into the third element of the touch of laughter, which is engaging in conspiracy that is good.

Conspiracy That Is Good

"If we sneak up behind this tree, we might see that little squirrel eating his nut. Shhh! Come on!" stealthily whispers the father as he waves his hand in a forward motion for the troops to follow. Little James and seven-year-old Tracy scamper behind their crouched father, pretending to be a woodsman scouting out the frontier wildlife.

"Let's spy on him and see where he hides his nuts!" conspires the father to his willing and eager young accomplices. The thrill of trying to silently sneak up on a squirrel in the backyard is an intriguing adventure to small children. Engaging in conspiracy that is good involves three factors: constructing harmless exploits, using secretive words and actions, and becoming coconspirators.

Constructing Harmless Exploits

First, the adventure or exploit is harmless in itself. Peeking at a gray squirrel eating an acorn in the backyard is about as harmless and safe as an activity can be. Good conspiracy usually involves exploits that have child-safe action or suspense built in. The natural nervousness of the squirrel makes his behavior jittery, unpredictable, and exciting to children. The children may squeal with excitement as they scamper after the retreating squirrel, chasing him up the oak tree.

The wise adult will encourage such enthusiasm and will participate in it. "Quick! James, go around to the other side of the tree! There he is! Do you see him?" coaxes the father as they all tree the little squirrel whose chattering, twitching scorn makes it very clear who really won the chase.

"Well, kids, he's a smart little critter. That's the way wild animals are. We'll have to try to peek at him another day," concludes the father as he walks back to the house with arms resting lovingly on the small shoulders of his children on either side of him.

The unpredictable, out-of-the-ordinary action made the exploit exciting. It was not thrill or suspense arising from something unpredictably dangerous or frightening. Most youngsters want to run after things. Whether it's a squirrel in the backyard, pigeons at the park, or seagulls on the beach, children love to make a game of trying to tag or touch them. Join in the excitement! Better yet, be childlike and instigate the fun!

Creative exploits can be skillfully engineered by adding make-believe to a commonplace event or even a work assignment. A little boy's bubble bath filled with floating toys can easily become a tankful of fish surrounding the friendly boy whale who tries to catch them while splashing to get squeaky clean.

An armload of warm clothes from the dryer may be dropped on young children relaxing in the family room. Feigning anxious concern, the adult may say, "Help me! Help me, quick! They're still warm and alive, but we've got to fold them before they cool down!" Pretending the load is something other than clothes from the dryer may catch the children's interest. Make believing they are alive and need taming into neat individual piles may stir the children's willingness to do a chore.

Of course, a child can take a bath or fold clothes without the conspiring touch of laughter. In fact, it is unrealistic and unhealthy to try to turn every event in a child's life into a game. Life is not like that, and you shouldn't pretend that it is by indulging the child with endless pleasurable activities.

Using Secretive Words and Actions

Let's go back to the father and children chasing the squirrel in the backyard. This harmless exploit is really an adventure laced with suspense. The father whispers, moves stealthily, and pretends to be spying. The children's natural curiosity, enthusiasm, and movement are purposefully subdued and momentarily contained by the adult. Why? To heighten the suspense and pique their childlike spontaneity to full expression. The children literally burst from their concealed hiding place and chase the little squirrel up the tree.

The conspiring touch of laughter capitalizes on natural intrigue and skillfully constructs intrigue by using secretive words and actions. The father's saying, "Shhh, be quiet! Let's spy!" is purposeful intrigue aimed at triggering the children's interest. The father's hand signals and crouched position that imitate a woodsman in hiding arouse the children's curiosity.

The conspiring touch of laughter may be secretive without being playfully cunning, as with sneaking up on a squirrel.

Conspiracy that has the secrecy element may be simply that—a secret.

Becoming Coconspirators

Good conspiracy with its secretive exploits involves fellow or joint conspirators. The adult or the child might be the leader of the creative adventure. The idea is that both share full involvement and are equal accomplices.

"Hey, Dad! See Mom and the girls? Let's sneak up as close to the picnic blanket as we can before they see us! OK?" ten-year-old Bobby playfully suggests to his dad as they are returning from the mountain lake with the freshly caught trout. The wise father will agree to carry out the adventure if at all possible. The child is thrilled to coax his parent into following him in a harmless exploit, and he thinks, *Gee, Dad, you're one of us.*

If Bobby's younger brother catches up to him and the father, the second son is included in sneaking up on the female family members. There is to be no rigid or fine line of separation between who can join in the fun and who cannot. Inclusion is to be the rule of thumb to those who desire to be part of the exploit. However, participants should be taught to take turns and to learn the concept of waiting at times.

Preparing to Sound the Depths

Catching the spirit of creative play is vital. Communicating the kindred, capturing spirit in a relationship with your child bonds you and your child more securely. Yet, however determined you may be in capturing the spirit of creative play, you must successfully deal with two factors before heart communication will occur. Chapters 6 through 8 explore these factors and discuss how you may sound the depths of your child's heart.

Part 2

**Powerful Forces
Surrounding
Creative Play**

Creative Play— Childish or Childlike?

"Out! What do you mean he's out?" yells the overly excited Little League coach as his son stands up, after attempting a steal to third base, brushes the red clay off his jersey, and slowly walks back to the dugout.

"You're blind! He was safe by a mile!" angrily shouts the disappointed father as he impatiently paces up and down the sideline. Then throwing his baseball cap to the ground in disgust, he stomps onto the field for a heated confrontation with the umpire.

We've all seen those out-of-control adults behaving with impulsive childishness because their will was challenged, angrily contesting another's decision because they didn't get their way.

Childish Behavior

The adult's fear of being perceived as foolish is a powerful inhibitor to willingness to engage in playful creativity. Childlike activity may be confused with childishness and be shunned.

Childishness is the innate, immature response that characterizes human behavior when one is faced with disappointment. Conduct, foolish and inappropriate for an adult, may spring as an instantaneous reaction when one's desired will is crossed by another.

Childish behavior may occur over a widely diverse range and vary from harmless, overt silliness to hurtful, explosive hostility. Regardless of the type of behavior or its intensity, most recognize childishness when it occurs and would prefer not to be guilty of practicing it. It is humiliating to lose self-control either in overdone silliness or in a red-faced shouting match. The fear of being foolish causes most adults to shun practicing either extreme or, if they do have a childish lapse, to feel shame for the undignified behavior.

An adult's hesitation to be creatively playful may be removed by a correct understanding of the difference between foolishly immature behavior and commendably childlike behavior. The Bible condemns the former as conduct unwise to emulate and as an example of naivete. But Scripture commends the latter as conduct worthy to emulate and as a mark of true maturity.

Looking closely at childish and childlike behavior will help clear up the confusion. For the adult's sake and, more important, for the child's sake, the adult needs to behave maturely when playing with the youngster. The negative impact of a childish, forceful adult is one of the surest ways to effectively shut down good communication with a child.

The Foolishness of Children Is Unwise to Emulate

Name-calling, grabbing, and other immature antics identified with childish behavior are secretly—and even openly—practiced by far too many adults.

What exactly is childish behavior, and what causes it? What is it about childishness that most adults seem to want to avoid or want to hide the fact of practicing?

Can a person become more mature in behavior when the irritating, exasperating moments occur that threaten to unravel dignity and self-control? Is there a reliable and accurate criterion by which attitudes, words, and actions may be impartially judged as wise or foolish for a person to practice? Yes! The Bible is an excellent and reliable guide for answering these questions on proper conduct.

Matthew 18:3 and 1 Corinthians 13 identify the underlying reason creative play so profoundly touches the heart of a child. They establish the biblical basis, the taproot that nourishes and flourishes good communication.

In Matthew 18:3–4, Christ commands adults to emulate childlike qualities as evidence of true spiritual maturity. He says, "Unless you are converted and become as little children, you will by no means enter the kingdom of heaven. Therefore whoever humbles himself as this little child is the greatest in the kingdom of heaven." In 1 Corinthians 13, the childlike qualities are identified so that adults may know exactly what attitudes and behavior they are to emulate. These qualities are gracious humility, sincere teachability, joyful righteousness, and trusting vulnerability, and they will be discussed in detail later. Practicing childlike attitudes and behavior is connected to honorably responding to God's authority. The childlike adult properly respects authority while the childish adult finds that difficult to do.

Creative play is based on the adult's practicing in an imaginary activity the very real spiritual qualities Christ commends him to demonstrate in real life. The young child, who initially and naturally possesses these spiritual qualities, senses an identity with the adult. The adult speaks in a language the child knows and understands. The adult creatively plays in a manner in which the child feels an identity and likeness—a kindred spirit that captures her heart and causes her to want to be closer to her parent.

Let's look at how the adult moves from being childish and begins to capture the spiritual childlike qualities commended by the Lord.

The Childish Adult Must Grow Up and Become Childlike

The immature adult is someone whose thoughts, affections, and conduct are marked by a failure to do away with childish things. It is someone who cannot say, "When I was a child, I spoke as a child, I understood as a child, I thought as a child; but when I became a man, I put away childish things" (1 Cor. 13:11).

What *things* are to be done away with? Preceding this great love passage is a single statement that is pivotal to understanding the concept of childishness: "I show you a more excellent way" (1 Cor. 12:31).

The childish adult refuses to recognize or regard anything greater or more important than herself; she fails to do away with centering herself as the best, most excellent, and correct authority in a given situation.

Principle #1:
Grow Up by Honorably Responding to Authority

"Off the field!" bellows the impassioned umpire, and the angry Little League coach is expelled from the game. Walking with embarrassed, awkward strides, he shakes his head in disgust and heads for his pickup in the parking lot.

The first basic principle in avoiding immature attitudes and behavior is learning to recognize and honorably respond to authority; it is respectfully acknowledging the rightful authority of another.

The great love passage of 1 Corinthians 13 makes a profound declaration in the first three verses. True maturity involves regarding with honor and appropriately responding to an authority outside oneself. The verses begin with noteworthy examples of the height of a person's spiritual, emotional, and physical maturity. However, when honorable regard of and response to a higher authority (the love of God) are missing, such attitudes and behavior are denounced as the worthless and deceptive performances of a foolishly immature and spiritually bankrupt person.

Why are such seemingly good intentions and actions counted as nothing—as foolish? A realm of authority other than oneself is to be recognized and considered, and from it originates the true measure of rightness. It is the more excellent way of honorably responding *first* with love and obedience to God and His authority then demonstrating love toward others.

The foolish and spiritually immature adult primarily regards himself first and believes that he is the mark from which attitudes, words, and actions are measured and judged right. Basically, the childish adult will disregard God and His authority in regard to righteousness and assume a false self-authority from which rightness is measured. Someone who does not honorably respond to another's authority will squarely position himself in his own mind as the most important factor to be considered in a given situation.

What does all this have to do with identifying and avoiding childish conduct in one's life? This same refusal to honorably respond to another's authority allows a child to mistakenly believe herself to be the primary and deciding factor in circumstances surrounding her life. This concept promotes a child's immature, self-centered thinking and behavior, and it is precisely what adults are challenged to put away lest they be guilty of emulating childishness.

Adults have more practice than children in acknowledging and regarding, whether willingly or unwillingly, higher authorities over themselves. They have lived longer and have had to do it more often. Whether the experience has been positive or negative, spiritual or nonspiritual, most recognize the wisdom and truth of doing away with childish thinking, reasoning, and speaking when they become adults.

The foolish notion that one's understanding and perception constitute the final word and authority on a matter is to be replaced by a willingness to honorably consider and respond to the rightful authority of another. In regard to human relationships, should there be opposing or contesting viewpoints, the issue should be discussed and resolved with appropriate acknowledgment and honor given to the one in charge.

In regard to the relationship with God, He is to be honored as the highest authority. We are to respectfully defer and obey. All of our thinking, feeling, and behaving is based on partial, finite knowledge and human experience while God possesses perfect and total understanding. Indeed, we think, reason, and speak in part, "but when that which is perfect has come, then that which is in part will be done away" (1 Cor. 13:10).

The first basic principle in avoiding immature behavior is to recognize and respond with respect to rightful authority. Childish attitudes and behavior ignore showing such respect. Of course, unprincipled obedience to every authority goes beyond what is required. Rather, one is to honorably respond rather than disrespectfully attack or ignore such authority, whether it is righteous or unrighteous.

Some of the greatest examples of true adult maturity occur when one honorably responds to an unjust human authority. The disciples' firm and respectful statement to an ungodly human authority's command to be silent about Jesus is repeated by the mature believer: "Whether it is right in the sight of God to listen to you more than to God, you judge. For we cannot but speak the things which we have seen and heard" (Acts 4:19–20).

We are to follow Christ's example, "'Who committed no sin, nor was deceit found in His mouth'; who, when He was reviled, did not revile in return; when He suffered, He did not threaten, but committed Himself to Him who judges righteously" (1 Peter 2:22–23).

Whether it is an irate coach verbally and abusively challenging an umpire's call or a disrespectful child adamantly refusing to obey a parent's bedtime command, each is demonstrating dishonor toward a rightful authority. This disregard will inevitably produce an immature display of childish attitudes and behavior in young and old alike. The mature adult has begun to grow up by learning to honorably respond to authority. Whether or not that authority is right or wrong in its decisions does not excuse the adult from responding with respectful and appropriate attitudes, words, and behavior.

Playful creativity will inevitably be affected in a negative way if the adult behaves with a childish disrespect for authority in real life. The adult's tendency to dominate, challenge, and have his own way in real life will constantly spill over into the playful pursuits he is trying to share with his child. The adult who is immature in showing respectful honor to authority in real life will most likely also demonstrate the most childish behavior in play. His habit of arguing and demanding his rights in real life makes him less of a good companion and friend in a playful situation.

Therefore, the more immaturity the adult displays, the greater are her risks of driving her child away in the relationship. Generally, a childish adult is a poor participant in an activity. The sooner the adult "puts away" her improper responses to authority, the sooner she will connect with her child's heart in real life and in creative play.

Principle #2:
Grow Up by Pursuing the More Excellent Way

Immature conduct occurs when one refuses to honorably respond to authority or when one refuses to pursue the more excellent way in dealing with others. Childish attitudes and behavior may easily occur between equals or peers in a given situation. A disagreement may rapidly disintegrate into an embarrassing and angry shouting match if one of the adults does not consciously follow a more excellent way in resolving differences.

Adults pursuing the more excellent way of love will inevitably become more caring and godly in real life. They will become more loving best friends and companions to their children. The more excellent way of love draws loved ones closer whereas immature responses of a childish adult drive loved ones away.

What exactly is the "more excellent way" referred to in 1 Corinthians 12:31? In 1 Corinthians 13, the more excellent way is revealed. The qualities of a mature individual are identified as the childlike qualities Christ commands adults to emulate.

The four elements of the more excellent way are found in verses 4–7 of 1 Corinthians 13:

> Love suffers long [is patient] and is kind; love does not envy; love does not parade itself [is not arrogant], is not puffed up; does not behave rudely, does not seek its own, is not provoked, thinks no evil; does not rejoice in iniquity, but rejoices in the truth; bears all things, believes all things, hopes all things, endures all things.

Element #1: Gracious Humility

"One for you and one for me," counts out Peter in deep concentration as he carefully places the red M&M in his little sister's hand and the green M&M in his own.

"Daddy, fix it for me please," expectantly asks his little daughter as she holds out her favorite doll and its broken arm.

The first element of the more excellent way is gracious humility. The child knows how to graciously give and to humbly look to another rather than make arrogant and bold assertions of personal greatness or ability.

Love that is God honoring and truly mature is patient and kind, which are the gracious aspects, and is not envious or puffed up, which is the humble aspect. Possessing gracious humility is closely related to whether one will demonstrate either childish immature pride or true childlike and praiseworthy attitudes and behavior in a situation.

Christ commended the gracious humility of a child and admonished adults to emulate this childlike quality. To what was Christ responding? He was correcting His disciples for their impatient, unkind jealousy and arrogance after a "dispute arose among them as to which of them would be greatest" (Luke 9:46; Matt. 18:1).

Gracious humility may be forgotten as a child's self-centered tendencies are practiced. Some children may be allowed such early prideful expression in their attitude and behavior that it may appear they never possessed this quality in the first place. Though image bearers of God, young children may not necessarily reflect more clearly this endowed quality. An adult's temperament or deep spiritual commitment may cause gracious humility to reflect in every area of his life. Whether present to a lesser or greater degree, how do you increase the inner quality of gracious humility?

Learn to focus on the highest authority figure: God. A focus on God helps keep a self-centered focus from taking place. The one who has a misplaced emphasis on himself will most likely display a haughty attitude toward others. Remember, when Christ's disciples stopped focusing on Him, they began to arrogantly argue who was the greatest among them.

Gracious humility is developed in the heart and mind of the adult as he consciously purposes to direct attention, thought, and affection toward another rather than toward himself. True spiritual maturity is grown in the adult who is "looking unto Jesus," (Heb. 12:2) rather than looking unto himself. The mature adult does not merely look out for his personal interests; he looks out for the interests of others (Phil. 2:3–8).

Gracious humility is the first element of the more excellent way, and the more an adult recaptures this childlike quality, the less likely that adult will display the childish and immature quality of unkind, presumptuous pride. True spiritual maturity is a direct result of a person's obedience to the higher authority of God's Word when it says, "All of you, . . . be clothed with humility, for 'God resists the proud, but gives grace to the humble'" (1 Peter 5:5).

Element #2: Sincere Teachability

"Class dismissed!" announces the fifth-grade teacher, and the joyful, newly liberated eleven-year-old students scurry out of the classroom door on the last day of school.

"Grampa, show me how!" pleads the fascinated nine-year-old as he watches his grandfather's agile, skilled hand trick of losing the peanut under the three walnut shells.

The second element of the more excellent way is sincere teachability. Children know how to respond with enthusiasm and willingly learn new and exciting lessons. Love that is God honoring and truly mature "does not behave rudely" or "seek its own," which is the sincere aspect, and "is not provoked," which is the teachable aspect.

The mature adult demonstrates a sincere willingness to learn a lesson and appropriately respond to its truthfulness. Sincere teachability is profoundly illustrated during Christ's triumphal entry into Jerusalem.

As Jesus descended the Mount of Olives, His followers began "to rejoice and praise God with a loud voice, . . . saying: 'Blessed is the King who comes in the name of the LORD!'" (Luke 19:37–38). This sudden, unrehearsed acknowledgment concerning the truth of Christ resulted from "all the mighty works they had seen" (v. 37). The followers' conduct was enthusiastic, a little less tempered by usual adult dignity and clearly pleasing to the Lord. Their genuine childlike sincerity of heart in responding to truth was spontaneous and acceptable.

The disciples' joyous declaration, "Blessed is the King who comes . . . ," showed their teachability. Christ commended them for the correct acknowledgment when He said, "I tell you that if these should keep silent, the stones would immediately cry out" (Luke 19:40). The implication is that if living humans were that unresponsive to such truth, the inanimate creation would be compelled to speak and declare it.

When He spoke the above words, to whom was Christ responding? He admonished the adults present during the triumphal entry who did not possess sincere teachability. He chastened their hardened refusal to acknowledge what was truly obvious. Lacking sincere teachability, they became "[easily] provoked" and unbecomingly demanded their own way. They insisted that the Teacher rebuke His disciples into silence (Luke 19:39). Supposedly mature leaders, they demonstrated a childish, unwilling attitude, refusing to believe truth and remaining rigidly unmoved in responding to it. The childish adults continued their condemning attitude, criticizing the children for singing "Hosanna" in the temple. And they indignantly demanded, "Do You hear what these are saying?" (Matt. 21:15–16).

Again, Christ commended the childlike, though perhaps a bit unorthodox, sincerity of heart of those responding to the truth concerning Him when He said, "Out of the mouth of babes and nursing infants You have perfected praise" (Matt. 21:16). Truth may be hidden from the supposed "wise and prudent [intelligent]" but be revealed to babes (Luke 10:21).

The adult who desires to practice the more excellent way must grow up in the ability to be teachable, to perceive truth and respond with God-honoring sincerity of heart. He is to be a mature thinker "who [is] of full age, . . . who by reason of use [has his] senses exercised to discern both good and evil" (Heb. 5:14). Mature adults are "no longer [to] be children, tossed to and fro and carried about with every wind of doctrine, by the trickery of men" (Eph. 4:14). Rather, they are to "grow up in all things" (Eph. 4:15).

The childish adult refuses to grow up because she refuses to practice a willing heart readiness to learn and embrace truth.

Instead, she pursues a selfish willingness to unbecomingly demand *her* own way rather than a willingness to understand and learn the *right* way. Generally, people most guilty of sinfully demanding their own way will be most provoked at the righteous expressions of the sincere of heart.

The expressions of the sincere of heart may vary over a wide range. However, a person's sincere expression is to be based on what is truthful and pleasing to the Lord. Christ Himself rebuked the sincere, though inappropriate and unrighteous, attempt of the disciples to keep the children from bothering Him. He said, "Let the little children come to Me, and do not forbid them; for of such is the kingdom of God" (Luke 18:16).

Sincerity of heart is always to be united in allegiance with God-honoring truth. The mature adult recognizes the vast difference between sincere, uninhibited responses to what is right and the impulsive or licensed display of sinful attitudes and behavior.

The second element of the more excellent way of love compels the adult to have a willing and teachable heart sincerity toward truth. The more the adult possesses the quality of sincere teachability, the less likely that adult will display the childish and immature quality of stubborn and resistant ignorance.

Element #3: Joyful Righteousness

"Pat him gently on the head this time," patiently instructs the five-year-old as he guides his baby brother's eager fingers in a light stroke over their dog's shaggy fur.

"If you kiss it and say you're sorry," prefaces the teary-eyed little girl as she cradles her scraped finger and lets her twin sister get a closer, apologetic look.

The third element of the more excellent way is joyful righteousness. Children generally have an inner sense of what is fair, right, and equitable, and they show a ready willingness to forgive when the offender expresses sincere concern or repentance. Love that is God honoring and truly mature "rejoices in the truth," which is the joyful aspect, and "thinks no evil" and "does not rejoice in iniquity," which are the righteous aspects.

The truly mature adult delights in what is honorable and good. He possesses a joyful, uplifted attitude, and there is a quality of God-honoring wholesomeness in what he approves and pursues.

Basic to acquiring the joyful aspect of love is practicing sincere forgiveness for any wrongs suffered. Thinking no evil or not taking into account or harboring ill will toward another is foundational to possessing joyful righteousness. Christ said, "Father, forgive them, for they do not know what they do" (Luke 23:34).

The mature adult chooses the greater joy of having a renewed or reconciled relationship over harboring ill will. The immature adult chooses to tightly clutch her angry, unforgiving attitude, much like a selfish child refusing to share a toy with another. The childish adult will not release the real or imagined guilty one from real or imagined offenses, choosing rather to tally up hurt, grievance, and animosity toward the offender. Accounting of wrongs suffered often leads to an angry, vindictive attitude and will thoroughly drive joy from the human heart. The adult choosing to pursue the more excellent way of love will purpose, by the inner strength that Christ supplies, to forgive as she has been forgiven (Eph. 4:32).

The righteous aspect of God-honoring love is intricately related to truth. Apart from objective truth, there is no basis upon which to evaluate whether attitudes, words, and actions are righteous. Without an objective and trustworthy foundation, everyone will do what is "right in his own eyes" (Judg. 17:6), often to the corruption and destruction of his and others' lives.

The childish adult bases the rightness of her attitudes and behavior on her finite and subjective perception and shows less accountability or allegiance to a higher standard than her own. Scripture points out the folly of measuring ourselves by ourselves and warns that those who do seldom come to an accurate evaluation of the truth: "But they, measuring themselves by themselves, . . . are not wise [are without understanding]" (2 Cor. 10:12).

Why is it without understanding when one does this? Human reasoning is capricious and inconsistent. Christ illustrates its inherent fallacy when He states,

> But to what shall I liken this generation? It is like children sitting in the marketplaces and calling to their companions, and saying:
> "We played the flute for you,
>   And you did not dance;
> We mourned to you,
>   And you did not lament."
> For John came neither eating nor drinking, and they say, "He has a demon." The Son of Man came eating and drinking, and they say, "Look, a glutton and a winebibber [drunkard], a friend of tax collectors and sinners!" But wisdom is justified by her children (Matt. 11:16–19).

Christ exposes the unreliable and untrustworthy nature of human reasoning when not based on the higher, more excellent, and right standard of God's truth.

The mature adult no longer thinks and behaves with childish, inconsistent reasoning. He rejoices with and seeks to adhere to God's revealed truth as the basis for his personal standard and practice of righteousness.

The third element of the more excellent way challenges the adult to joyfully respond in recognition of and allegiance to God's standard rather than a personal standard of truth. The more an adult possesses this quality of love, the less likely that adult will display the childish and immature quality of presumptuous, unforgiving self-righteousness.

Element #4: Trusting Vulnerability

"I said one stick of gum, not the whole pack!" exclaims the big brother in disbelief as he stares at the large round bulge misshaping his younger brother's right cheek.

"OK, if you promise to hold him carefully," agrees the concerned seven-year-old as she gently places the dwarf gray-and-white hamster in her father's large calloused hand.

The fourth element of the more excellent way is trusting vulnerability. Though children are naturally vulnerable, they willingly give themselves over to the care, help, and protection of another. Love that is God honoring and truly mature "bears all things" and "believes all things," which are the trusting aspects, and "hopes all things" and "endures all things," which are the vulnerable aspects.

The truly mature adult honestly reveals and shares who he is out of love for another. With self-disclosure comes the inherent danger of being hurt or rejected. The one who chooses to love with trusting vulnerability is willing to risk possible physical or emotional pain. He values the relationship more highly than his personal sacrifice.

The supreme example of trusting vulnerability is Christ Jesus. He did not withhold Himself from a relationship with humankind. He "made Himself of no reputation. . . . He humbled Himself and became obedient to the point of death" (Phil. 2:7–8). Like Christ, the mature adult willingly empties herself by not selfishly holding on to an advantage and by making herself more transparent, approachable, and accessible to others.

The aspect of trust is seen when one gives something of significance to the care of another. Love that "bears all things" and "believes all things" demonstrates the ultimate entrustment of oneself to another. Love that pursues the more excellent way must be resting in a heart allegiance to and reliance on God rather than on humans because basic inadequacies and failings make uncertain any human foundations.

The mature adult chooses God as the basis for what he is to believe and bear whereas the childish adult selects a human-created foundation on which to base his belief and shoulder his efforts. Scripture demonstrates the eternal value of resting beliefs and efforts on the sure foundation of God and His Word when it points out that Christ, who "committed Himself to Him [God] who judges righteously" (1 Peter 2:23), was also "highly exalted" for what He believed and bore (Phil. 2:9). God and His Word provide a sure foundation on which mature people build their lives and share in relationships with others.

The aspect of vulnerability is seen in the more excellent way of love when one "hopes all things" and "endures all things." Christ's steadfast endurance accomplished God's will of salvation and also demonstrated the awesome extent to which Christ willingly chose to become vulnerable. Laying aside His sovereign deity, He became incarnate with the limitations of human flesh for the purpose of reestablishing a loving and whole relationship.

The mature adult not only hopes for but also actively pursues a loving relationship with others; she is willing to endure being vulnerable if that is what it takes to communicate vital messages to the hearts of loved ones.

The fourth element of the more excellent way reveals the depth of commitment necessary to win another to a loving relationship. The more an adult possesses this quality of love, the less likely that adult will fail in efforts to make sincere and real heart contact with others.

Maturing and Becoming Childlike
Are Inseparable

The most completely balanced and mature adult ever to live is the Lord Jesus Christ, and He commands adults to emulate the faith and example of the young (Matt. 18:3). Resting your faith in Christ begins this process, and pursuing the more excellent way of love continues your process of growing up and becoming more childlike and truly mature.

Maturing and becoming childlike are inseparable. As would be expected, there is a profound effect in your life when you become more graciously humble, sincerely teachable, joyously righteous, and vulnerably trusting. Not only is a profound change being made in regard to you personally, but also a profound impact is being made on persons to whom you relate.

Desiring to secure a loving relationship with your child, you will find that a special bond of recognition takes place in your child's heart when you begin to emulate childlike spiritual qualities. When you express the spiritual qualities of the young, ready lines of communication are more open between you and your child's listening and attentive heart.

A legitimate question can be raised at this point. You may understand, accept, and truly desire to emulate the childlike qualities of the more excellent way. But you may be asking, How exactly do I do it? The answer is found in correctly determining where and on whom you are resting your deepest heart concerns.

If you trust yourself and your effort to make right a relationship, you will probably do well in improving that relationship by the simple fact that you care and are willing to work on communicating with more loving skills. However, if you trust in Christ to make right your eternal relationship with God, you will likely seek Christ's help in improving a temporal, human relationship. You will probably do even better in revitalizing your human contacts because you possess God's enabling Spirit within, "who works in you both to will and to do for His good pleasure" (Phil. 2:13).

The four elements of the more excellent way lay the foundation on which you, as a mature adult, will build a strong relationship with your child. As your character and personality are shaped by them, your young child readily identifies you as more like himself because he innately possesses these qualities, too. Even an older child will significantly and more readily identify with you because these spiritual qualities are a part of her brief life history.

The more excellent way of love is available for you to implement in your life and relationship with others. The quality, extent, and duration of any improvements in a relationship may significantly vary, based on whether you rest your efforts on yourself or God. In either case, human hearts will be lovingly touched by your conscious and sincere effort to make emotional contact with loved ones.

When you unite the spiritual qualities of gracious humility, sincere teachability, joyful righteousness, and trusting vulnerability with the natural physical qualities of your child, the message of love, identity, and acceptance rings loud and clear in the heart of your child. But before learning to weave fun and imaginative games around those qualities, you need to deal with another major factor that inhibits good relational communication. In chapters 7 and 8, discover how to authoritatively and creatively defuse power struggles.

CHAPTER 7

Defuse the Power Struggle by Creative Leadership

"Nap time, Jenny," calls the mother as she walks through the back bedroom, gathering up the discarded clothes piled on the floor by her active three-year-old. Picking up a sock, she loudly instructs from the hallway, "Jenny! Jenny! I said it's nap time. Go potty and get in bed now."

Her daughter, having just snapped the last button to her doll's gown, pretends not to hear and continues playing house on the sofa.

"Jenny! Jenny! Did you hear me? It's nap time. Come right now!" impatiently repeats the mother as she enters the living room. Irritated by her daughter's delay, she reaches out one free arm to take Jenny by the hand.

"No!" Jenny says defiantly. "I don't want to!" And shoving her mother's hand away, she tightly clutches her doll, refusing to budge from the couch.

The drama is set; the players are positioned; the power struggle begins. It's an age-old power struggle that threatens to destroy endearing relationships between parent and child. Adult and child pit themselves as antagonists, ready to do battle. With each ensuing conflict, the feelings of camaraderie, goodwill, and playful creativity gradually extinguish.

"You're taking a nap!" shouts Jenny's mother. Grabbing Jenny by the arm, she angrily yanks her to the bedroom, depositing her screaming daughter in a heap on the comforter.

"No! No! No! I don't want a nap!" sobs Jenny, uncontrollably kicking her legs and thrashing in the tangled sheets.

What has gone wrong? What is a parent supposed to do? Recognizing that power struggles will recur in varying degrees during the lifetime of a relationship puts a proper perspective on the situation. Every age level will likely have struggles. You need to successfully handle and defuse conflicts, not ignore them.

Understanding three basic principles will help you accomplish this. Chapter 7 deals with the authority issue, which is the first principle. Chapter 8 discusses the second and third principles in regard to being creatively playful.

Principle #1: Establishing Proper Adult Authority

Two concepts regarding authority will help you do your parenting job better. The first concept deals with how you are to *be*. The second concept deals with what you are to *do*.

Be Lovingly Authoritative

"No! You can't because I said so!" blurts the irritated father responding to his ten-year-old daughter's repeated pleas to go bike riding after supper.

"Just do it! Don't ask me again!" demands the weary mother calling for the third time to her young son to get out of the swimming pool and dry off.

One assumed parental idea is expecting the child to automatically obey. Reasoning that parental words and actions should not be challenged or questioned, the parent commands, is ignored or refused, and then becomes angry with the child's resistance.

It is good to expect obedience; however, you must teach it to your child. Properly handling authority helps win your child's heart obedience to your leadership. How you are to be lovingly authoritative is the issue facing you concerning the challenging task of successfully raising your child to honor God.

God knew how hard that would be for you, so He gave a perfect example of how to be lovingly authoritative in the person of Jesus Christ. To defuse the power struggle between you and your child, become a Christlike role model of authority.

Becoming a Christlike Role Model of Authority

What is a Christlike role model of authority? It means patterning the way you exercise your authority after the manner that Christ exercised His authority. The more excellent way of love will affect every level of your leadership.

Basically, authority is someone's influence being exercised in regard to another. Human authority based on the principles of God's truth keeps childish tendencies more under control. The more excellent standard of God's authority imposes guidelines and restraints.

Human authority based on reasoning apart from God's standard is fallible. The criteria for right and wrong, good and bad, become subjective, relative, and arbitrary. Human authority begins exercising its power and control by doing what is right in its own eyes (Judg. 21:25). Human authority becomes childish by not honorably responding to the higher authority of God's standard.

Can Authority Be Christlike and Childlike?

Christ condemned powerful leaders for their misuse of authority when He said, "Laying aside the commandment of God, you hold the tradition of men. . . . All too well you reject the commandment of God, that you may keep your tradition" (Mark 7:8–9). They "pass by justice and the love of God" (Luke 11:42) for the sake of adhering to foolish human reasoning, which is false, hypocritical, or unnecessary.

The fallacy of human authority not based on God's standard was exposed by Christ when He said, "The kings of the Gentiles exercise lordship over them, and those who exercise authority over them are called 'benefactors.' But not so among you; on the contrary, he who is greatest among you, let him be as the younger, and he who governs as he who serves. . . . I am among you as the One who serves" (Luke 22:25–27). Christ made that declaration to His followers after He washed their feet, and "there was also a dispute among them, as to which of them should be considered the greatest" (Luke 22:24).

The principle of becoming a Christlike role model of authority rather than a childish role model of power is beautifully illustrated as Christ brings home His point of true mature rule. He says, "Do you know what I have done to you? You call Me Teacher and Lord, and you say well, for so I am. If I then, your Lord and Teacher, have washed your feet, you also ought to wash one another's feet. For I have given you an example, that you should do as I have done to you" (John 13:12–15).

The mature adult exercises his authority based on the standard of God's Word rather than on the standard of human self-centered and childish reasoning. His influence and control are modeled, conformed, and accountable to God's truth and thereby transformed more into a Christlike role model of authority because of God's sovereign influence. The more excellent way of love vitally impacts his rule, attitudes, and behavior.

The childish adult wields her authority without higher, biblical constraints and directives on her conscience, will, and actions. In her mind her attitudes and behavior are justifiable because they feel and appear right, good, or equitable; they seemingly are the best accomplished means to an end in a given situation.

The alignment of human reasoning with God's wisdom should not be attributed to any intrinsic rightness in human thinking. Rather, God has implanted within every human heart an instinctive, felt consciousness of His law (Rom. 2:15), and the extent that a person abides by or denies that divine persuasion determines whether his attitudes and conduct will be more childlike or childish in expression.

The adult is to grow up and become a Christlike role model of authority in the same manner Christ demonstrates His mature authority. True leadership is living out the more excellent way of love as Christ did. He received authority: "All authority has been given to Me in heaven and on earth" (Matt. 28:18). Christ obeyed God's standard. He declared, "I always do those things that please Him [God]" (John 8:29). Christ modeled God-based authority with its commendable childlike qualities. As the most influential leader ever to live, He graciously invites, "Come to Me, all you who labor and are heavy laden, and I will give you rest. Take My yoke upon you and learn from Me, for I am gentle and lowly in heart, and you will find rest for your souls. For My yoke is easy and My burden is light" (Matt. 11:28–30).

The adult who takes seriously God's command, Christ's example, and his responsibility to become a Christlike role model of authority will truly become a more mature leader. He will more effectively connect with the hearts of those over whom he has influence.

Authority and True Communication

The adult who understands and attempts to become a Christ-like role model of authority will begin practicing this mature behavior in the significant relationships of her life, especially to-ward her child. As the adult begins to discard childish ways of interacting and replacing them with the childlike ways of com-municating, her authority will become more receptive to the heart of her youngster. A leadership opportunity opens up that profoundly affects the relationship.

The parent has awesome power to influence when he begins thinking and behaving with childlike spiritual qualities in his life. Children identify with those qualities because they possess them. The power struggle takes on a whole new dimension. The child perceives the adult as one who truly understands and identifies with the child. The adult becomes less a forceful tyrant who dominates or a lenient incompetent who has no control and more the beloved friend who leads well.

Why does a Christlike role model of authority communicate better than a childish role model of power? To bring this con-cept to life, let's pretend to be invisible witnesses when a mother responds to a child's misbehavior.

At the park, two mothers push their infants in the swings and chat about how big their babies have grown. Suddenly, one of the two small children playing in the sandbox beside them grabs the other's bucket and shovel and refuses to give them back. "Mommy! Mark took my things. I want them! Mommy!" cries his little playmate.

A childish heavy-handed response from Mark's mother would sound like this: "Why can't you ever be nice and share? Give that back to Jimmy right now!" Leaving her baby, she hurries to the sandbox, grabs the shovel and bucket from her son's hand, and shakes him painfully by the shoulder before giving Jimmy back his things. "Be nice!" she angrily reminds her crying son. Leaving the sandbox, she walks back to the swing, shaking her head in disgust at her son's bad behavior.

A childish lenient response from Mark's mother would sound like this: "Give the bucket and shovel back. Mark, are you listening to me? I said to give them back, now! Do I have to come and get them? I'm going to count to ten and you better do it!" The mother's monologue may slowly prompt Mark to return the playthings but more than likely she too will become angrily embattled with her misbehaving son.

A childlike authoritative response from Mark's mother would sound like this: "Mark! Give Jimmy his bucket and shovel right now!" Leaving her baby, she walks to the sandbox and takes the bucket and shovel firmly, but gently, from her child's hand and returns them to his little playmate. "Mark, don't take Jimmy's things again. If you do, Mommy will have you sit beside me by the swing for five minutes. Hey! Look! Let's make a big fat sand-man with twigs for arms! I'll dig some sand to get you two started," she offers as she piles up two handfuls of white sand in a mound. "Be nice," she reminds in a friendly tone before returning to her baby in the swing.

Notice the gracious manner of the authoritative response. The mother gently removed the toys from her son's tight grasp. She warned him of her future correction if he did not immediately alter his misbehavior. If correction did become necessary, the consequence, though a sorrowfully felt one, was not harsh or excessive.

She attempted to divert her son from further misbehavior by a joyous emphasis on a creative activity and by a gentle reminder to be nice. The mother encouraged a teachable quality in her son by demonstrating a patient and compassionate response in her manner. By her very words and actions, she became someone he could emulate and model. The mother allowed herself to become vulnerable by inviting her son and the other child to join her in the fun of building a sandman. The mother willingly left herself open for possible rejection because restoring a good relationship was more important than keeping a nominal peace.

The mother's sincere attempt to demonstrate the spiritual qualities of a child while carrying out parental authority in correction served her well. More than likely, the child will wholesomely respond to the mother's friendly and creative redirection rather than experience a sorrowful correction. The mother greatly improved that possibility when she positioned herself as a loving and good companion to her young son. Should he refuse her instruction and continue in misbehavior, the mother has positioned herself as a loving and authoritative leader who is most definitely in charge of her child and who will most definitely correct his disobedience. The child's perception of his mother, whether he willingly obeys or challenges her authority, is one of wholesome respect for her because she has exercised her authority as a good companion who leads well.

How do you learn to handle parental power correctly? How do you behave with authoritative leadership? How do you not sinfully "provoke your children to wrath" but instead "bring them up in the training and admonition [instruction] of the Lord" (Eph. 6:4)? These questions lead directly to the second underlying concept to defusing the power struggle by establishing proper adult authority: What are you, as a loving authoritative parent, to *do*?

Correct with Love and Authority

The key to exercising mature authority is to emulate Christ's childlike example of leadership; the key to exercising mature correction is to pattern parental discipline after God's correction of His children.

What you, as a mature adult, are to do is to teach your child the right way of behaving by lovingly correcting misbehavior. Two of the most significant scriptural passages that reveal the heavenly Father's parental attitude and action toward His children are Psalm 103:8–14 and Hebrews 12:5–11. As an authoritative parent, you will sincerely attempt to emulate the compassionate parental attitude set forth in these verses:

> The LORD is merciful and gracious,
> Slow to anger, and abounding in mercy.
> He will not always strive with us,
> Nor will He keep His anger forever.
> He has not dealt with us according to our sins,
> Nor punished us according to our iniquities.
> For as the heavens are high above the earth,
> So great is His mercy toward those who fear Him;
> As far as the east is from the west,
> So far has He removed our transgressions from us.
> As a father pities his children,
> So the LORD pities those who fear Him.
> For He knows our frame;
> He remembers that we are dust (Ps. 103:8–14).

As an authoritative parent, you will sincerely attempt to emulate the corrective action set forth in these verses:

> And you have forgotten the exhortation which speaks to you
> as to sons:

"My son, do not despise the chastening of the LORD,
Nor be discouraged when you are rebuked by Him;
For whom the LORD loves He chastens,
And scourges every son whom He receives."

If you endure chastening, God deals with you as with sons; for what son is there whom a father does not chasten? But if you are without chastening, of which all have become partakers, then you are illegitimate and not sons. Furthermore, we have had human fathers who corrected us, and we paid them respect. Shall we not much more readily be in subjection to the Father of spirits and live? For they indeed for a few days chastened us as seemed best to them, but He for our profit, that we may be partakers of His holiness. Now no chastening seems to be joyful for the present, but painful; nevertheless, afterward it yields the peaceable fruit of righteousness to those who have been trained by it (Heb. 12:5–11).

Training a Child from an Authoritative Perspective

One of the best ways to defuse the power struggle between a parent and a child is to lovingly train and correct from an authoritative perspective. That is how the heavenly Father trains and corrects people He loves.

Molding a child's lifelong character involves training with purpose and direction. The following steps, based on the verses from Psalm 103 and Hebrews 12, are the foundations of authoritative discipline.

However, before you look at the steps, you need to consider several points:

• You need to believe with conviction that correcting your child is not an option to be exercised occasionally and only under duress; it is a consistent, wholesome, and daily occurrence to be administered in a loving manner.

• You need to establish reasonable house rules that clearly define acceptable and unacceptable behavior and that consistently administer consequences for misconduct and rewards for obedience.

• You need to consider the age and maturation of your child and match the child's age and offense with reasonable correction.

• You need to have a loving attitude to accompany your clearly defined expectations.

These steps help you get a handle on how to correct your child's misbehavior but not crush the spirit. Being aware of and applying a positive and consistent correction method will greatly enhance your ability to creatively play with your youngster.

———

We have had human fathers who corrected us, and we paid them respect. Shall we not much more readily be in subjection to the Father of spirits and live? (Heb. 12:9).

The command. It initally begins the expression and exertion of your authority in a situation. Give your command clearly, precisely, and lovingly to your child so that there is no confusion or misunderstanding about your instruction. The child's cooperation is encouraged by your loving manner of rule. Give the command in a friendly tone unless an immediate danger or emergency prevents that.

You can't presume that your child can read your thoughts and follow your unstated directives. God informs His people very clearly and precisely about His commands and expectations. To defuse the power struggle between you and your child, you should work at being just as clear. But what if you are clear and loving with instructions, and your child hears, understands, and still refuses to obey? What do you do then?

————

The LORD is merciful and gracious,
Slow to anger, and abounding in mercy. . . .
For He knows our frame;
He remembers that we are dust (Ps. 103:8, 14).

The warning. You give a grace period to your beloved child, much like the Lord extends a grace period to His children. The warning is a gentle, though firm, reminder to a wayward child that a disciplinary action will occur if he doesn't correct misbehavior.

Generally, the warning may be issued up to three times; however, it should not be threatening or frightening. It is a clear, loving caution to the child that unacceptable behavior must be altered more along the appropriate lines you have set. You may even choose to remind the child of the consequences of not obeying. For example, saying, "Melissa, you must sit down in your high chair, or Mommy will have to correct you," is a gentle, firm reminder to a small child.

————

"My son, do not despise [regard lightly] the chastening [discipline] of the LORD,
Nor be discouraged when you are rebuked [reproved] by Him;
For whom the LORD loves He chastens. . . ."

Now no chastening seems to be joyful for the present, but painful [sorrowful]; nevertheless, afterward it yields the peaceable fruit of righteousness to those who have been trained by it (Heb. 12:5–6, 11).

The correction. You should consistently correct your child for misconduct. God does, and you would do well to follow the heavenly Father's example. Correction may be administered physically or nonphysically in a variety of ways. The child may feel appropriate physical correction when having to sit quietly for a specified amount of time, being held securely on your lap, or being sent to his room. The child may feel appropriate non-physical correction when listening to the parents express displeasure and disappointment during a talk time, losing a reward or privilege, or performing a job as restitution. All correction should have as an initial part a felt consequence which is sorrowful. Correction that is unfelt either emotionally or physically is a useless token of true correction and makes a mockery of a parent's authoritative training.

Your choice of correction is consistent with your overall knowledge of your child. The correction is a firm but compassionate expression of your commitment to bring well-being and good to your child. A child's temperament, constitution, health, heredity, past and present experiences, and environment are all contributors to who he is.

Administer felt discipline while keeping the child's uniqueness in mind. Try to be compassionate and understanding of your child's shortcomings and weaknesses.

———

> He will not always strive with us,
> Nor will He keep His anger forever (Ps. 103:9).

The comfort. You should be the first to extend comfort to your child if you administered the correction. As the authority figure who administered the felt sorrow, you should be the first to soothe the child's temporary hurt or sadness. The heavenly Father who corrects the disobedient through discipline is also the first and most willing One to "heal the brokenhearted" (Isa. 61:1) in their sorrow. He is willing to be the first to communicate His continual love and care for those who have been wayward.

Some people mistakenly reason that this is inconsistent behavior—first correcting and then soothing the child. Remember, the parent is to administer brief felt consequences—not harmful, long-lasting emotional rejection. It is unhealthy double correction to withhold comfort from a child who has just experienced discipline.

The comfort phase allows the child to complete momentary grieving in the arms of his parent who loves him dearly. It also helps to reveal whether or not true repentance has occurred in the child's heart. A child who angrily stiff-arms away from you and refuses to be comforted probably has not experienced a truly significant felt consequence, or if he has, he is either unrepentant over his misconduct or belligerent for some reason. All of these are good reasons for you to further investigate the problem.

Whatever the cause, the comfort phase allows you time to evaluate the effectiveness and correctness of the discipline. It also provides an opportunity for you to sympathize with another's sadness and hurt.

As a father pities [has compassion on] his children,
So the LORD pities [has compassion on] those who fear
   [reverence] Him (Ps. 103:13).

The prayer. Seek to help your child willingly respect your authority. The prayer allows your child to have a peek into the type of cooperative relationship you desire of her. By praying and asking the heavenly Father for help, you acknowledge your submission to a higher authority.

You also demonstrate personal accountability to that higher authority. You model the correct submitted attitude and behavior toward authority that you expect from your child.

You might say, "Lord, please help Larry obey me, and please help me be a loving parent to my precious son." You may wish to include your child by inviting him to pray, also. If he is unwilling to pray, don't force repentance, a prayer, or an apology from your child. "I'm sorry!" gritted through the clenched teeth of a child makes a mockery of expressing true repentance or asking forgiveness.

Rather, let the example of prayer for your child stand as the loving witness of your willingness to be submitted to a higher authority than yourself. You can always pray for your child without the child having to pray himself.

———————

For as the heavens are high above the earth,
So great is His mercy toward those who fear [reverence] Him;
As far as the east is from the west,
So far has He removed our transgressions from us
(Ps. 103:11–12).

The restoration. This is the final step in authoritative correction. As the Lord does, so the parent is to welcome back a once disobedient child into the warmth and comfort of a restored relationship. Rather than allow an issue or incident to be never ending, properly settle the matter in the correction step and focus on resuming normal family life.

You might justly argue that if your child is not penitent or the relationship is not restored, what can you do then? The restoration step is your actual visual attempt to be reconciled with your child: "Alex, I know you're still angry that you were corrected. I want you to know that I corrected you because I love you. I'm not angry with you. [Or I'm working on my anger, and I hope you will work on yours.] Whenever you want to come outside [or any pleasurable invitation] I would love for you to be with me." This is a natural, loving attempt at restoration. You can't force your child to be reconciled, but you can always choose to be reconciled in your heart toward him.

Generally, your child will desire to be emotionally and physically reestablished with you. Therefore, the restoration step is to be your gracious attempt to positively repair the temporary breach in the relationship. It is to be a signal that the incident is justly settled, the matter is satisfactorily closed, and as far as you are concerned, family life may again resume—perhaps on a more amiable note.

Your child may or may not accept your gracious overtures. Regardless of your child's response, you are setting the pattern for true restoration by extending an invitation for the relationship to be made right.

Proper Correction and a Child's Deepest Longings

Properly settling the authority issue significantly defuses the power struggle between parent and child. The parent lovingly and firmly communicates a vital message that touches a profound inner longing of the child: "Love me enough to lead me." One of the deepest heartfelt desires of a child is to know that she is loved and that she is accountable to the one who loves her. A parent who establishes firm, compassionate, and consistent authority communicates love and a commitment to work for the child's well-being.

To take such time and effort, you must love and value me greatly, instinctively reasons the child. The child's sense of feeling loved and secure is further confirmed in her mind when she challenges the adult's authority and it does not crumble. A child who destructively strains to win the power struggle will feel emotionally insecure if she does win, further fueling the vicious cycle of tension and uncertainty in her relationship with her parent.

A child desperately wants to know that someone bigger and stronger than himself is there to love, lead, and protect him, even from the tyranny of his willful, selfish demands. Properly settling the who-is-in-charge question communicates the parent's commitment of love for the child and encourages the child's wholesome respect for adult authority. A lovingly authoritative parent will attempt to win the child's heart by being a Christlike role model of leadership. This very style of relating will defuse the power struggle that much of the time needlessly occurs between parent and child. The child identifies his parent as one under the authority of Christ in the very real matters of leadership and correction.

Now, let's turn our attention to the other profound way by which you may defuse the power struggle within a family. Chapter 8 discusses the creative, playful way.

Defuse the Power Struggle by Creative Play

The Great Untapped Gold Mine

There is another highly effective means of defusing the power struggle between adult and child. Like the discovery of rich treasure just below the ground's surface, your discovery and use of creative play will greatly enrich the lives of family members.

Creative play helps you keep balanced in your interaction with your child. Keeping a measured sense of goodwill and compassion for childhood antics goes a long way in winning your child's repentance and obedience from the heart.

There is a broad range of acceptable creative play, and it will be influenced by your personality and background; however, you will model good humor, fair play, and respect if your actions are appropriate.

Chapter 7 dealt with the first principle of defusing the power struggle. Now let's examine the second and third principles.

Principle #2: Be a Good Role Model of Companionship

Besides being a good role model of authority, you need to learn how to be a good role model of creative and playful companionship. To creatively play, recognize and master the skills of a good child communicator. Usually, good child communicators make good child companions.

"And the scampish little blocks tried to hide from the big toy box, but we caught every one of them and put them all away!" pretends the mother as she weaves a story of building blocks trying to escape capture by the mother and the child while they are picking up the child's messy bedroom.

Cleaning a room, preparing a meal, and going to bed are all wonderful occasions to interact with a child and build a relationship of companionship. Relational communication does not occur only when you are trying to be relational, such as reading a bedtime story or helping a youngster learn to ride a two-wheeler. Relational communication is to be experienced throughout the child's day.

Good companions tend to share and enjoy activities in common. Children like to be playful and creative as they express their ideas or carry on an activity. How do you become a good companion and communicator with your child?

Share Your Lighter Side

Put aside unnecessary adult seriousness. Is it difficult for you to really romp with your little one? Is it hard for you to participate in make-believe by telling a nonsense story or imagining a fantasy game? Are you able to make fun out of work? Do you often belly laugh with your child or playfully tease him by an unexpected, out-of-the-ordinary surprise? If these thoughts are unfamiliar to your way of thinking, you are probably too serious in your parental attitudes and responsibilities.

This is not to suggest that you act like an overgrown kid who does not know how to leave childhood behind. Being an expressive childlike companion is not relinquishing your parental role in the life of the child. You may need to get more authoritative and in charge of your youngster before attempting to creatively play. The child who perceives you *only* as a companion and equal is at great risk of becoming a disrespectful and undisciplined child.

Good companions share things in common, and most adults are capable of playfully sharing an idea, game, or adventure with their children if they will release that little child within. Learning to lighten up is to share yourself—your past and present—on an expressive, relational level with your youngster.

How you share your lighter side is important. Remember the mother at the sandbox in chapter 7? As a Christlike authoritative leader, she blended the natural childlike qualities of playfulness, spontaneity, imagination, curiosity, and motion with correction. She lightened up the corrective aspect of her leadership with youthful expression. Being silly is different from being youthful. The former prevents the adult from being taken seriously while the latter communicates messages in a friendly and receptive manner. To share your lighter side, you must first recognize the natural qualities of children and then blend those traits with the spiritual qualities of children.

Recognize and Emulate the Natural Qualities
of Children

Understand the natural, physical characteristics of childhood, and work creatively *with* rather than *against* these qualities. Some of the most basic natural traits of children are playfulness, spontaneity, activity, imagination, and inquisitiveness. It is vital to your relationship with your child to discard any aspects of a grown-old mentality and rediscover your dormant youthful expression.

Most children intuitively know how to be playful, spontaneous, active, imaginative, and curious. The degree of their involvement and expression may vary tremendously due to heredity, personality, and environment. Some children seem naturally expressive while others appear lifeless in contrast. Do not be overconfident or discouraged because your child leans one way or the other.

The mature Christlike adult establishes good emotional contact with her youngster by recognizing and emulating these physical traits. She will be a keen observer and copier of the child's forms of expression—especially the playful, creative ones. "Hey, Sweetie! Tickle me off the couch, if you can!" may be the mature mother's invitation to play.

Blend the Natural and Spiritual Qualities
of Children

Blending the natural and spiritual qualities of children occurs in the routine affairs of family life. At mealtime, bathtime, bedtime, play, or work, the creative adult captures opportunities to blend these qualities and connects with the child's heart more securely.

Let's return to the example of the mother correcting her young son playing in the sandbox. She demonstrated being a childlike role model of authority as she exhibited the spiritual qualities of the more excellent way while correcting her son. She was gracious, righteous, and vulnerable as she dealt with the situation. She was correctly in charge of her child while at the same time being a loving leader and companion.

Did you notice the physical manner in which she handled herself? The mother attempted to emulate the physical qualities of her child. She was active, playful, and imaginative while positively redirecting her child from teasing his little playmate. Her body language was expressive and youthful; she got down on her knees and heaped up white piles of sand. Her ideas were creative; her imagination surfaced when she thought up the idea of making a sandman in the first place. Her words were enthusiastic. She talked playfully.

Because the mother thought, acted, and talked with the natural qualities of a young child, she likely communicated her authority and friendship more clearly to her son. She blended some of the spiritual qualities of gracious humility, sincere teachability, joyful righteousness, and trusting vulnerability with some of the physical qualities of playfulness, spontaneity, imagination, curiosity, and motion for a winning combination.

Creative blending of the physical and spiritual qualities of children occurs best as you learn to recapture youthfulness. Becoming a childlike role model of companionship involves learning to think young and to act young. Good child companions do both.

Think Young by Recapturing a Good Sense of Humor

Why can Grandpa's storytelling, with whispered mystery in his voice, spellbind the grandchildren in hushed silence? He weaves a tale of the good old days, his eyes twinkling with delight as he describes the mishap with the watermelon. Creative, imaginative thinking gives animation and enlivens youthful enjoyment and expression regardless of chronological age. That is why some older people are so exciting and alive in spirit and some young people are so uninteresting and colorless in personality.

The secret of a good child communicator is to think with creative youthfulness. Learn to think young by associating with young thinkers—children. Some of their positive childlike characteristics have been mentioned: playfulness, curiosity, spontaneity, imagination, and activity. By sincerely living out these qualities, you will go a long way in significantly defusing the power struggle in your relationship with your child. Chapters 9 through 11 teach you how to actually practice these qualities in creative play; for now it is important to grasp the general concept of learning to think and act youthfully.

Think Young by Reclaiming Your Childhood

Reclaim some of the wholesome, playful attitudes that you possessed as a child. Enjoy both past and present childhood adventures with your youngster.

Telling of past joys and wholesome occurrences of your childhood gives your child colorful access to your past and helps you not to take yourself or your child too seriously. "Well, Jason, after I caught that stray dog and got back my pants, I was all sweaty again and jumped back in the pond for another swim," chuckles Dad as he remembers that hot day in August when he was ten. Good humor is relived, loved, and laughed at by adult and child alike, and the relationship of companions is felt and shared.

You can learn to appreciate and enjoy present humor by observing things from a child's perspective. Crawl under your dining room or kitchen table, and peer out from behind the tablecloth from the eye level of a child. The adult world looks huge and intriguing when observed from three feet off the floor. You can see mysterious cabinet doors to be opened and searched; chairs and tables appear as tangled trees to crawl through.

This is not to advocate allowing your child to do whatever her inquisitive and sometimes naughty little mind thinks up. However, if you see, experience, and appreciate things a little more from your child's perspective, perhaps you can see some of your child's foibles with more humor. Good companions are able to share a good sense of humor over the everyday activities and mishaps of life. They are friends through it all.

Act Young by Laughing

One of the most vital ingredients to acting young is being able to truly laugh with good-hearted pleasure and enjoyment. Good-humored laughter can range from the hearty belly laugh to the playful smile. Positive laughter enhances creative expression and builds true companionship between parent and child. Negative laughter destroys any feelings of creativity or playfulness and effectively tears down a relationship.

Positive laughter is not directed unkindly at a child or his efforts. "You put those on your mother's valentine!" says Dad, unsuccessfully concealing his sarcasm and amusement as the little five-year-old proudly hands his mom the homemade valentine pasted over with yellowish weeds. Good-humored laughter enfolds the child, and he is endeared for his efforts. "Oh! Jason, it's beautiful!" exclaims the mother with pleased affection, sniffing deeply the weeds. And her mouth curves in a smile as she reads the card.

Act Young, Not Silly

Creative playfulness does not automatically imply silly behavior. Measure whether playful activities are creative and wholesome by observing whether or not the positive natural qualities of children are being expressed.

Playfulness will remain within healthy boundaries and not become out-of-control rowdiness. Spontaneity will be safe and not become dangerous or harmful impulsiveness. Imagination will be creative but not a delusory detachment from reality. Curiosity will show politeness rather than be a rude invasion of privacy. Motion will be laced with action but not become harmful, painful, or frightening.

Good playful activity can subtly develop to permissive silliness or rudeness if you are not alert to some signs of immature behavior. If an activity becomes an embarrassment to the child, the adult, or others, usually someone is behaving immaturely rather than creatively. People are generally uncomfortable and embarrassed when someone speaks too loud or with coarse jesting that communicates a mean or immodest attitude. Though there may be laughter and seeming tolerance and acceptance of such behavior, the more base, negative side of humor is being demonstrated rather than the wholesome, positive side of creative humor.

Actions can become inappropriate displays of silliness or rudeness if the parent or the child begins acting immodestly or becomes uncontrollably rowdy. People generally want to avoid excessive rowdiness because of the possibility of someone's getting hurt. A well-meaning father may become too rough in playful romping with his child, and the wrestling match ends sadly with a child in tears clutching a hurt knee.

How else may you defuse the power struggle between you and your child? A third principle defuses conflict, and it is also a playfully creative method of relating.

Principle #3: Become a Team Player

The concept of a good companion is taken further as you position yourself as a team player in your child's wonderful and exciting adventure called childhood. What does it mean to be a team player in your child's life? First, let's consider what game is being played, and second, let's discuss how you get on the team.

The Game of Childhood

Understanding some of the natural and healthy childlike attitudes and actions that young children bring with them into life sets the stage. Being too strict or too lenient spoils a child's spirit and may damage the zeal for engaging in the game of childhood.

The game of childhood is not to be taken as some unrealistic but interesting label being put on the very serious business of raising children. The game mentality does not refer to immature or negligent behavior on the part of the parent. It means that parenting and childhood can be just as exciting as any intriguing game of skill, wit, or adventure. Perceiving something as a delightful activity has the psychological effect of lifting one's spirit and lightening the load of responsibility.

Who Is on the Team?

Perceiving childhood as a wonderful and exciting growing-up game is one piece of the puzzle. Recognizing that the parent and the child make up the team is the other piece.

Gaining a team spirit means that you regard your youngster's childhood as a shared experience. Since play is such a vital part of your child's world, your willingness to play shows that you have a greater amount of team spirit.

How to Be a Team Player

You need to be a good team player before you can be an effective team leader. You need to send the message, "I'm willing to play with you, and I want to play with you," before trying to lead your child in a creatively playful activity. The parent who seldom wholeheartedly participates with his child in a structured activity will probably find her confused, resistant, or unresponsive if he suddenly attempts to lead her in a creatively playful activity.

This is merely a caution so that you don't become discouraged if your good efforts and intentions are, at first, received less than enthusiastically by your child. A child is so resilient and accepting that he will generally respond with energy and delight when shown playful parental attention. Most often, your efforts at being playful and creative will be welcomed and glady received by your child, who deeply longs for your expressions of love.

For you and your child to be good team players in a game, certain things need to occur in real life. As discussed earlier, you should be a good role model of authority. Being lovingly authoritative in real life sends a winning signal to your child. You communicate openness to being receptive, playful, and friendly in a game because you demonstrate these qualities in real life.

The child who cooperates with the parent in real life will more wholesomely and enthusiastically engage in a game of creative play. He has learned to respect boundaries and practice more self-control, so he is free to focus on the fun and the game rather than on how he is to behave when playing.

The child who demands and is allowed to be in charge in real life will become a forceful and demanding team antagonist whenever things do not go exactly her way in a playful game.

Since her attitudes and actions often angrily challenge and disregard the parent's real commands, she will also try to take charge of her parent and control the parent in a game. An unsubmitted or uncontrollable child makes an aggressive team antagonist rather than an enjoyable and delightful team player.

A team player is more than a companion. For the adult and the child, team players are companions who properly relate in real life and playfully engage in the adventurous game of childhood.

Let's see how the adult can become a wonderful team player with the child in the exciting game of growing up.

Grandmother Putting Todd to Bed

As good team players in real life, Todd knows to respect and obey authority, and his grandmother is lovingly authoritative and in charge of him. Now in a creative game, they both engage in fun as team players.

"Todd, let's read this story about the rascally mouse before you go to sleep," suggests the grandmother to her six-year-old-grandson. She selects the brightly illustrated book about the naughty mouse who tries to snitch food from the lazy yellow cat.

The grandmother pitches her voice high and squeaky, pretending to be the little mouse trying to swipe the cheese from the cat sleeping by the fireplace. As she reads, "I got it!" from the story, her hand becomes the gray mouse trying to escape the awakened cat.

She pretends to hide her hand under Todd's bedsheet and pleads a frightened, "Help me!" Her hand begins tickling Todd as her fingers scamper all over his arms and legs, trying to escape the meowing cat who has somehow jumped from the storybook pages and is chasing the naughty little mouse all over Todd and the bed.

"Grandma! Stop tickling me! Hee! Hee! Hee! Get away!" squeals the laughing youngster as he wiggles frantically to tuck the bedsheets tightly under his body.

"Get away? What are you talking about, Todd? I was reading this story, and you start jumping around! What's gotten into you, Sweetheart?" playfully asks the grandmother, resuming the mouse adventure as if nothing unusual happened.

She may repeat the mouse episode several times while progressing through the story. As the grandmother nears the end of the book, she may again pitch her voice high and squeaky as she says, "Well, good-bye, little boy. I loved playing with you! Thank you for saving me from the big cat! Please pat me before I go home."

Quietly moving her hand near the child, the grandmother pretends it is a good mouse, not a rascally, tickling one. She snuggles her soft hand against the child's cheek, strokes his hair, and encourages him to playfully pat her hand as if gently touching a soft little animal.

Being a companion and team player means that the adult equally enjoys and invents relational activities that are creative and playful. The adult demonstrates youthful thought and action; the fun and adventure of growing up are shared together as the adult positions himself as someone on the team in a fun-filled and exciting way. Being companions who are good team players in childhood will defuse the real-life power struggle. When outward relational communication occurs, emotional bonds are developed and strengthened.

Playing the Games

Now, putting all this together, it is time to play make-believe games and learn how to have creative fun. Chapters 9 through 11 teach you to construct imaginative games and discover the delight and wonder of connecting with your child's heart in the process.

Part 3

**Make-Believe
Games
Weave
Hearts Together**

Make-Believe Games of Companionship

"Now let's tuck these pillows all around and snuggle you under the blanket," invites the mother putting four-year-old Daniel to bed. She shapes the four soft pillows into what looks like a cozy round nest in the middle of the child's bed. Then fluffing up the warm blanket as if she is feathering her make-believe nest, she says, "There! Everything is ready for my little baby bird to be all comfy and warm on this cold, windy night. Hop in without a peep and I'll get some storybooks to read before you go to sleep." Then she bends her arms at the elbows and flaps them like a mother bird flying away as she walks to the bookshelf.

More than likely, the child will bounce up on the bed, wiggle into his nest, and chirp like an excited, impatient baby bird waiting to be fed. For the mother and the child, a make-believe game of companionship has begun.

What Is a Companionship Game?

Does that conversation and activity stir a faint hint of the familiar, a sweet remembrance of some loved one doing something similar and dear with you as a child? You remember the wonderful, tender moment, the special feeling of closeness, the person wove a web of love around your heart and you never forgot it.

Companionship games weave the heart of the parent and the heart of the child together as best friends. They are your conscious attempts to "knit together in love" the heart of your child with your heart (Col. 2:2). As a loving and encouraging parent, you seek to win your child over to a closer relationship. As a godly parent, you will in turn win the child over to a closer relationship with the Lord.

Companionship games are playful inventions of the mind, creative, imaginative ideas put into action. You and your child share these activities in such a way that each expresses inner youthfulness and childlike qualities. Let's use the baby bird illustration at the beginning of this chapter and discover two basic elements of all companionship games. The third element, which vitally connects the first two, will be discussed in chapter 10.

Two Basic Elements of Companionship Games

The two basic elements of creative make-believe games are (1) the adult and the child are companions (2) who are together in a playful activity. Companionship games are powerful influences in a relationship if they are accompanied by the parent's sincere attempt to daily relate well to the child.

Be a Companion

Who are companions to the child? The child's family members, other significant adult friends, older children, and peers are all possible companions. For games of companionship, the best friend concept is usually shared among members of the immediate family (parents, grandparents, aunts, and uncles). It may be used by extremely close family friends, or it may be modified to include other significant adults (a Sunday school teacher or youth leader). Children who are near in age often naturally engage in make-believe games on their own initiative with their best friends.

If adults other than parents engage in the best friend concept, they must not compete with the parents. Any significant adults in the life of a child should attempt to be positive influences to encourage the wholesome and healthy bonding between parent and child.

How to Be a Companion Who Is a Best Friend

Being companions means that each player is regarded as a best friend or good buddy on the team. Whenever people desire a team concept in a relationship, certain factors and attitudes must be recognized to keep that concept alive and healthy.

One such factor is age. Generally, children like to play with other children who are near their own age. Usually, best friends are peers. In games of companionship, the adult is attempting to become a best friend with the child despite the significant age difference.

In fact, the age difference may promote successful bonding in a companionship game if you communicate as a best friend would. The natural built-in competitiveness between children who are peers is removed. In a game, you are not tempted to be

125

first, get the biggest, or say, "It's mine," or "It has to be my way," as young children are.

Let's return to the mother pretending to nest her child. The mother putting her child to bed positions herself as a caring mother bird patiently building something comfy for her energetic baby boy bird. The mother's animation makes it clear that her nestling is free to chirp and clamor like a real baby bird or be quiet like a good little human pretending to be a sleepy baby bird. Companions who are best friends give each other the freedom to be themselves within healthy boundaries.

"Yes," you say, "but what if my child doesn't respond like a sweet baby boy bird?" Creative make-believe games help you capture your child's heart. Childish problems will occur. Attempt to resolve them while winning your child's heart.

If the child responds with overly rowdy or silly behavior, she may feel uncertain how to creatively play, or she may be in a nonsensical mood. Gently instruct the child how to appropriately pretend to be a baby bird rather than give harsh or critical correction. As a good companion, you will be understanding.

"Sally, let's not throw the pillows on the floor. Little birds stay in the nest and chirp and flap their wings for attention, Sweetheart." Such a comment will direct her in being creatively playful without dampening her spirit.

A child's reasons for noninvolvement in your game cover a wide range from tiredness to disinterest and preoccupation. As a good companion, you will not push it. Good friends are free to express when they want or do not want to play. You might end on a pleasant friendly note by saying, "Oh, well, Sally, I guess you just don't feel like being a baby bird tonight. We'll play another time. I love you, Sweetheart."

Perhaps your child is belligerent in response to your attempt to play a make-believe game. Most likely, a hostile response indicates there is an underlying unresolved problem in your relationship. As a good companion, you will let it surface. Your friendly attempt at a make-believe game lowered your parental defenses in the heart and mind of your child. You became someone approachable and perhaps vulnerable and her true inner feelings toward you or a situation were allowed to surface. As a good companion, you will put the make-believe game on hold and address the real-life issue.

In effect, the nonthreatening game allowed your child to more easily open up in real life. Coax your child to further express her feelings: "Honey, what's the matter? You don't want to play because you're hurt or angry. What is it?" Good companions show that they care, and they try to help.

Sometimes a child starts out well playing a make-believe game and then gets overly rowdy, silly, or belligerent. Perhaps the child is attempting to get in charge of the situation, is responding with tired energy, or is trying to exclude a younger brother or sister. For whatever reason inappropriate behavior emerges, do not let it sour the outcome of the make-believe game and end on a negative note. As a good companion, you will attempt to reconcile any problem in the relationship.

You shouldn't allow a present problem to shadow creative and playful prospects in the future. "If you can't play right, we're just not going to do this anymore!" sends a death note to the heart of the child of joyfully anticipating the parent's involvement again. As a good companion, you will attempt to deal with the problem and will not hold a negative or permanent threat over the head of your child.

Be Together

Being together as good companions in a creative game is communicated in a variety of ways. You must learn to make your parental actions child friendly while playing.

The following communication skills will help you and your child feel that you are together, speaking the same language. These skills are specifically designed for make-believe games, though they work well when applied to real life.

Together by Invitation

In the baby bird companionship game, the mother winningly invites her child to join her. By pretending to be a bird, the mother signals to the child that a make-believe game is beginning. She reinforces this idea by pretending the pillows are a nest and her child is a baby bird. She does not say, "You have to play." She merely introduces the idea, then develops the fantasy seemingly just for the fun of it.

Games of companionship are most successful when the parent creatively draws the child into the activity, when the parent's manner communicates an invitation to the child to join in the fun. The child senses that he is developing the idea with his parent. The child is allowed to share in the fantasy, and the activity bears the stamp of his creativity as well as the parent's.

Suppose Daniel says, "Wait, Mom! The pillows need to be piled against the back of the bed like they're on a branch!" and he pushes them toward the headboard. The child's creativity is engaged and moving forward. Being together in a companionship game means that Mom will allow Daniel to re-create the fantasy more to his liking while using her ideas as a basis.

Together by Consent

Though the mother's invitation is friendly, it should be regarded as just that, an invitation. She suggests an imaginative and playful idea and attempts to put it into motion. The child is free to respond positively or negatively, with or without enthusiasm, as a participant or an observer. Demanding that the child engage in creative play because she wants him to take part is coercion, which won't capture a child's heart.

Asking, "Now, baby bird, do you want to stay in your pillow nest for a story?" allows the child to decide if he wants to engage in the make-believe game. The child is free to accept or decline the invitation to creatively play.

If he responds positively, the mother is at liberty to further weave a sense of togetherness: "Let's see. Is this nest big enough for me to hop in beside you, or should I just curl up real close next to you?" Either suggestion places the parent nearer to the child. Always attempt to create a win–win situation.

If the child declines the invitation to join in a game, the mother needs to accept the refusal graciously: "Oh, well, Daniel, sometimes little boys just don't feel like being baby birds. That's OK. I'll flap my wings and fly back to the bookcase unless you want Mommy to read one story before you go to bed."

Perhaps Daniel doesn't want to make believe a game because he feels the need or desire to communicate with his parent in real life. You see, at school today, he was embarrassed when a little girl in class laughed at his wrong answer to the teacher's question. In fact, the whole class laughed! His little heart is hurting, and he does not feel like playing. He feels like sharing a real need with his parent.

The parent's willingness to become approachable through a make–believe game helps to open up the child's heart. Through the companionship game, the child feels closer to his parent even though he declined to play. Daniel is much more likely to open up and tell his mother what is really on his heart and mind because she asked for his consent to be together.

Together by Intent

There needs to be a unity of purpose when playing a make-believe game of companionship. You and your child should have a sense of what is going on, a feel for the togetherness that you are attempting to communicate. This is not only a good communicative skill, but it is also a biblical one. For believers to function as a family of faith, Paul says that they are to be "like-minded, having the same love, being of one accord, of one mind [intent on one purpose]" (Phil. 2:2).

In regard to games of companionship, the intent is to bring you and your child together in a more wholesome and loving relationship with each other. To realize that intent, you and your child must function as a team in the playful activity.

Both need to recognize that the make-believe activity is just a game. It is an imaginative, playful game with no negative hidden messages or agenda. Each needs to feel welcomed by the other, and both are equally willing to play. Both need to feel a mutual ownership of the activity. Each willingly stays in character for the duration of the game. Each contributes a special part, which creates a sense of completing the whole. Both need to have the freedom to introduce the game and also bring it to a conclusion. Wholehearted and willing involvement of each is more important than doing an activity for activity's sake.

Decorate with Wonder

Creative make-believe is decorated with colorful ideas and expressions. A pageantry of wonder is painted before the eyes and mind of the child. The adult creates this sense of wonder by animation and accentuation.

The mother in the baby bird game pretended that the pillows and blanket were a nest and she and her child were birds. She stayed in character and created a make-believe event around the reading of a bedtime story.

"Why do all this? I'm a parent, not a performer," you might protest. Yes, you are a parent, but you want to capture your child's heart along the way. Cartoons and animation captivate young children and even older television viewers. When something is portrayed bigger than life as an intriguing adventure, the child's attention is engaged.

You are capable of spellbinding your youngster with imaginative expression and action in a playful setting. Be best friends; decorate your child's life with wonder.

Live the Fantasy

Creative make-believe games involve a person being imaginative *with* another, not *for* another. In the baby bird game, the mother got into the fun and fantasy. The idea is to playfully set aside who you really are for a moment. Instead of being a parental authority figure, you become an imaginative and playful companion with your child.

This does not mean that you take an unhealthy flight or escape from reality. Detachment from reality is a refusal to deal with real life. You choose to become creatively childlike for the purpose of building a better relationship with your youngster.

Coax Another's Creativity

In the baby bird game, the mother's animation was an excellent role model for the child to follow her lead and imitate creative behavior. A child catches the spirit of playful make-believe very quickly and usually wants to jump right into the fun. Coax your child's natural creative tendency by giving her cues along the way.

Coaxing a child with creative cues needs to be handled wisely. A child may take cues to inappropriate limits or directions.

Be kind and patient while gently correcting your child. He senses your willingness to interact even if he makes a mistake.

Lovingly Correct and Redirect

A creative make-believe game offers such a rich and fertile medium for the imagination that a child may easily become overly engrossed, active, or inappropriate in behavior while playing. Correct unacceptable conduct and at the same time enhance the game and keep it moving along.

One of the best ways to positively correct is to creatively redirect the child. The concept behind a creative companionship game is that the adult and the child are best friends together in a playful activity; they are a team sharing a make-believe game. By words and actions, you convey the idea that you and your child must work together as a team to make it, finish it, or win in the imaginary situation. Also, you can create more excitement by stacking several make-believe occurrences on top of each other.

Getting Started Smoothly

Now you need to get started. Your child needs for you to relate in a creatively playful manner with him.

Getting the feel for something is an important first step. Learning how to carry out that felt idea is another. The first two elements of the companionship game help you get the idea, the feel for playing a creative make-believe companionship game. Perhaps you are beginning to sense how wonderful and fun it would be to share in an imaginary adventure with your child, to draw close to your child in a heartfelt relationship and to be the one who creatively opened up her heart.

Companionship games have another element that enables you to truly communicate love, friendship, and acceptance to your child. Being companions together in a playful setting allows your child to emotionally experience the welcome, warmth, and security of your presence. However, the kind of playful activity will determine how well the child experiences this feeling. Will any game capture your child's heart? In creative play, the game saga is the vital link that joins you and your child as bonded best friends. Chapter 10 carefully examines the game saga and its importance to connecting with your child's heart.

Companionship
Game Sagas

The vital third element of the companionship game is
the game saga. It is visually and verbally weaving an
imaginary activity in such a way that the companions acting out
the activity feel a heart oneness. Doing a playful creative activity
gives tangible and real expression to that feeling.

The game saga provides a structure from which to interact.
It has two distinct parts: the game aspect and the saga aspect.
Understanding both will help you successfully master the ability
to creatively play with your child.

The Game Aspect

Companionship games should look, feel, and play like real
games with a beginning, a period of activity, and an ending.
Being creatively playful does not mean that you spend your

entire day trying to capture your child's heart through imaginative games. Companionship games are momentary reprieves, playful experiences, in the midst of your workaday world. There are three game aspects of a companionship game.

Game Aspect #1:
Natural Blending of Real and Make-Believe

"Stevie, let's buckle you into the cockpit and take off in our pretend plane!" suggests the mother as she settles her youngster in the car seat and securely snaps his seat belt.

The real-life drama of riding safely in a vehicle is blended with the make-believe adventure she is introducing to her son. There is a natural blending of activities. It is time to go, and Stevie needs to be secured in his car seat. The mother is adding a creative enticement to accomplish her real-life goal of getting Stevie settled for traveling. The touch of make-believe positively flavors what could otherwise be a distasteful event in the relationship between Stevie and his mom.

"Hold tight for takeoff, and fly your airplane carefully!" encourages the mother as she turns the ignition key and begins backing out the driveway. The mother does not introduce a make-believe game that would run counter to her intentions in real life. Fastening her child's seat belt is a very real and important task. The companionship game assists in accomplishing the normal routine while adding fun. Blending the real with make-believe adds color, creativity, and life to everyday and often monotonous activities.

Game Aspect #2:
Moving Through the Phases

Companionship games involve creative play rather than structured play. Structured play usually has more well-defined boundaries involving the beginning, the playtime, and the ending of the game. Companionship games do not have sharp, identifiable boundaries. The activity may be relaxed or active; it may be intertwined with household routines or nestled by itself into a few moments set aside for something special.

Beginning a creative make-believe game is easier than ending it. Your tone of voice, language, and animation signal that a fun, imaginary activity is about to begin. Your child will generally pick up on the slightest indication that you want to be creatively playful. Do not suppose that you have to make endless suggestions to interest your child in the activity. Offer a few. If your child does not respond or take an interest, forgo the activity until another time.

The playtime is just that, a period of time when you play. You should be ready and willing to be playful with your child. You should be there in mind, body, and spirit for the duration of the playtime.

Ending a creative make-believe game on a happy, emotionally bonding note requires skill. Since the boundaries between real life and a companionship game are not rigid, you are in greater danger of dampening your child's spirit when the game must cease and you must resume adult responsibilities. The following ways successfully conclude a special creative time.

Give Advance Notice

Give advance notice to your child that the companionship game will soon be over. Getting this news while still playing tends to cushion disappointment to some degree.

End with a Promise

To conclude a playtime, end with a promise. Pleasantly saying, "We'll play this again sometime," is an excellent way to close down an activity. Or you may affirm a promise with a big yes when your child pleads, "Can we play this again?" By ending with a promise, you signal your commitment to making more special times available to your youngster in the future.

Stop Before Someone Is Played Out

Any game, whether structured or creative, may be easily spoiled if any participant strongly desires a conclusion to the game while it is still being played. This is not referring to attitudes or actions that demonstrate a poor sense of fair play. "I'm tired; I want to stop!" whined by a four-year-old losing in a game of Candyland is an example of selfish unwillingness to play.

Most children need to develop the determination of sticking out an activity whether or not they are winning. However, you should distinguish between the spoiled behavior of the child and the very real need to stop when the activity is becoming counterproductive to the relationship.

Remain alert and sensitive to the child's involvement. If you have to prod your youngster to stay in character or interact, more than likely the game is played out and should be stopped.

You can take a reading of your child by recognizing the signs. Is the child's mind or attention wandering? Are his eyes focusing on something other than the immediate activity or action? Is she yawning or absentmindedly fiddling with an object out of boredom or disinterest?

Remember, there is nothing wrong with the child wanting to stop a make-believe activity because he has become tired or disinterested. Best friends who are playing a game together stop playing for all kinds of reasons.

It is your responsibility to pick up on your child's message of wanting to stop the game. Try to stop before the child verbalizes game-killer comments: "I'm tired! Let's stop! This is getting boring!" If you correctly read your child's nonverbal communication, you can successfully conclude make-believe games on a positive note.

Game Aspect #3:
Teaming Up

The game aspect of companionship games has one other element: teaming up. There is to be no competition between parent and child. They are a united body for the duration of the playtime.

This attitude permits minor playful skirmishes between the participants. In chapter 11, the concept of playfully pitting the child against the adult in a mock power struggle will be discussed. Playing that type of make-believe game is crucial in defusing the real-life power struggle between adult and child. But before mock battles can be staged, the adult and the child need to experience real bonded unity while playing a game. The companionship game that heightens a felt sense of teamed up unity between participants is an excellent way to promote relational bonding.

The game aspect is integral to creative play. In companionship activity, your child needs to feel she is participating in a tangible, though imaginative, game with you. She needs to sense that a special time of fun and sharing is being masterminded and invented by the two of you. However, the saga aspect is also important.

The Saga Aspect

The saga aspect of companionship games creates the memorable moment. It takes a commonplace experience and communicates a life-sustaining expression of love from you to your youngster. Sagas are dramatic episodes which capture your child's attention and interest in a fun-filled way. Sagas help identify the grown-up as the child's wonderful and exciting best friend.

Sagas Are Dramas

"We're coming really close to the rocks! Push hard! We're tipping over! Quick, grab on to the sides and hold tight, Tommy!" commands the father shaking the refrigerator box from side to side and pretending to push his broom tree branch against an imaginary boulder jetting out from the river rapids. Then leaning back hard, he almost tips the box over and bounces his little son into a giggling heap onto his lap.

The dramatic episode of running the rapids in a saga of adventure has begun for the parent and the child. The episode is crammed full of intrigue, action, and suspense. The box sways and moves with the swirling of the current. The imaginary rocks lurk dangerously on either side of the make-believe boat. The father and the son are desperately trying to keep afloat and ride the river to the frontier settlement downstream. In fact, the settlers are depending on them to bring in the winter supplies before the river freezes over! The pillows and the blanket in the box are really food staples, and the ragged teddy bear is their faithful dog accompanying them on this treacherous river run.

The drama in a saga is what brings it to life; it is the creative touches of make-believe that the adult and the child construct along the way. Let's look closer at capturing the spirit of being dramatic in a companionship game.

Personalize the Drama

Bringing drama to life involves getting personally into the adventure. It involves fantasizing real-life occurrences into the make-believe game and surrounding the imaginary with what is seemingly real.

Primarily, the dramatic element is conveyed by expressive voice intonation and mannerisms. More important than the objects surrounding the parent and the child is the adult's ability to dramatically construct intrigue through body language.

In the river rapid saga, the father enjoyed communicating excitement and adventure to his young son. He spoke descriptive words—"quick, grab, hold tight" with feeling, intensity, urgency. He looked excited! He sounded excited!

The dramatic element may be subtle or less restrained. It may be very, very quiet or very, very loud. For instance, in a different saga, perhaps where the father and the son are trying to elude a giant, the desired dramatic touches would be mystery, caution, and suspense. The father would communicate in hushed whispers and secretive signaling.

The father may say, "Shhh! Be real quiet! Be very careful!" or "Watch out! He'll hear us!" The adult places an index finger to his lips and tiptoes around the corner of the hall. Peeking cautiously at the decorative pillows on the living room couch, he pretends that the pillows form the sleeping giant he and his son are trying to elude.

The adult's intonation and mannerisms accent and embellish whatever dramatic effect he is attempting to create. The success of all the other creative touches depends on the adult's skill in being dramatic. The box boat in the river rapid or the pillow giant will do little to fire a child's enthusiasm or imagination if the parent is a disinterested, monotoned participant.

The dramatic effect is also heightened when an adult carries out actions that are characteristic of true-to-life movement. In the river rapid saga, the box really shakes as if in a whirling current; the father tightly grabs the box's walls as if to stay inside the rocking boat; the child really feels the box tip as if their boat is beginning to capsize.

Staying in character further develops the dramatic theme. The father may pretend he is the older, perhaps more experienced, frontier companion to his brave young partner. However, the adult does not talk down to the child. The father acts like both are seasoned river men fighting together against the rugged natural elements. The father may use riverboat terms, pretend an accent, or describe the wild country they are passing through.

The dramatic aspect in a saga usually involves multiple mock mishaps or dangerous situations because problems occur in real life. The mock trials and difficulties add reality and credibility, which further enhance the drama.

The saga should always end with the sense of having successfully made it through the adventure. The feeling that we conquered the hostile elements, we arrived safely at our destination, we won the battle together, concludes the saga on a positive note of affirmation. The dramatic effect of always making it helps to bond the parent and the child together on a successful team.

Drama in a companionship game enlivens the saga or fun activity because it is playfully experienced as make believe and as real life. While drama gives motion to the saga, another key part is the episode or story line in the activity itself.

Sagas Are Episodes

Though the episode aspect is not as outwardly exciting as the dramatic aspect, it is equally important. The episode is the imagined event, the plot, the story line, which gives meaning and shape to the drama in the saga. The episode is a creatively playful invention of the mind, which may or may not be true to life. The river rapid saga was an episode characteristic of real life. The sleeping giant saga was an episode characteristic of fantasy. But both sagas came alive when they were creatively played as if both were real happenings.

Learning to develop good episodes is crucial for you to successfully connect with your child's heart in a companionship game. Let's look at some elements that will help you positively communicate a good episode.

A Good Story Line

In all companionship games, whether quite complex or very simple, the episode is the event or happening around which the participants engage and interact. From elementary games with young children to complex adventures, something memorable occurred to the parent and the child. A make-believe story was creatively told and acted out in a playful manner.

The first basic element of a good episode is a story line, an idea that you want to creatively express. Though the story line is usually fleshed out as you and your child play the game, you need to have a general idea of the imaginative elements you wish to include in the saga. As in the river rapid saga, the father and the son pretended they were river men riding the rapids to a frontier settlement.

Impromptu ideas and actions should be encouraged and added as enhancements to the fun. The general story line can change during a companionship game, but it should not be so abrupt that the spellbinding effect is broken. Nor should the general story line be changed to comply with a child's unsportsmanlike behavior: "I don't want the box to be an old boat! I want it to be a house!"

Welcome and encourage impromptu ideas when your child genuinely expresses creativity. For instance, in the river rapid saga, the child may have a sudden burst of creative inspiration that makes him and his father Indians in a log canoe instead of river men in a boat.

To construct a good story line in the companionship game, you need to keep in mind several factors in regard to your child. Is the child too young or too old for the activity in the saga? Placing a one-year-old in a huge shaking box would probably frighten the child, and even suggesting playing together in a cardboard box would be more of an embarrassment than a welcomed delight to a thirteen-year-old.

Good story lines take into consideration the emotional needs of a child. In companionship games, even an older child longs to be singled out as special and shown affection in a creative way. Many companionship games that otherwise would be outgrown by a child because of chronological age may still be loved because of the continued need to emotionally bond.

Good story lines have a degree of truthful accuracy. That is, the make-believe activity is creatively interwoven with real facts of life. For instance, if a mother is pretending to bake mud pies with her four-year-old, she should pretend to measure out or really measure out the natural ingredients of sand, water, and leaves. She should smell, stir, and pretend to taste the concoction, finally pronouncing it ready to be formed into mud pies and baked on the rock oven. Embellishing reality adds to a good story line.

A good story line within the creative make-believe game helps you communicate your desire to interact with your child with endearment and fun. Story lines may be nonsensical or simple childlike ditties; they may be involved and intriguing dramas like the river rapid adventure. A good story line will communicate to the child the treasured sense of being especially singled out and loved by a caring adult.

Other Factors of Episodes

You need to take other considerations into account as you develop a good episode. One factor is the location or site of the game. Designate safe zones, and if necessary, literally mark them off. In our living room, couches and chairs have been physically moved out of the way so that more safe room could be given to a romping, wrestling, make-believe game. Also identify wholesome and reasonable boundaries beforehand so that someone or something won't get hurt.

Other factors are the time of day, your child's physical needs, such as eating and sleeping, and your child's unique personality and hobbies. Do not decide to creatively play with a hungry or tired youngster. Do not pick a make-believe adventurous episode that counters the child's personal likes and dislikes. The little daughter who loves pretending to be a ballerina probably will not be intrigued with a wild ride in a cardboard box.

Despite the point just made, however, the very real power of good episodes to influence a child's thoughts and responses to life may stretch the personal comfort zone. Perhaps the ballerina daughter needs to learn how to handle the tougher things that come along in real life. She experiences the fun and excitement of doing something a little out of character for her makeup. How do you expect your child not to become rigid in relational skills unless she keeps relationally limber through creative play?

To engineer a lesson in stretching your child's wholesome interaction outside her personal comfort zone, you could invite your daughter to accompany you in a canoe going downstream to a lonely frontier settlement. Pretend dangers may occur, but imagine how happy the frontier people will be to watch a beautiful ballerina dance for them once you and she arrive!

Good episodes along with good drama allow all kinds of companionship games to communicate the feelings of lasting friendship and closeness between you and your child. A dramatic episode has the power to influence your precious youngster to take hold with her heart your value system and teaching. It can capture her inner being to more readily acknowledge, accept, and emulate the godly truths you so want to pass on to her.

The Deeper Meaning Behind the Game Saga

A good dramatic episode in a companionship game teaches or communicates the heart messages that you desperately want to express to your child. The messages are countless, but some of them are, "I love you dearly! I want to understand you better! Listen to me. I care about you! Respect me. God says . . ." You have certain values and beliefs that you want to instill within your child. You want your child to wholeheartedly embrace these truths as a way of life. You do not want your child to just endure your values until he is outside the home and your influence. When a valuable message is lovingly communicated in a manner the child can hear, receive, and process, the parental message more easily becomes the child's belief.

Let's look at companionship games that weave good game sagas in a dramatic way so that valuable life messages are communicated to the heart of the child. Let's play make-believe games that teach a child to be kind to needy people, identify with a parent's positive role modeling, and develop a good work ethic.

A Saga Teaching Kindness Toward Others

Is your youngster playing house in the backyard? Why don't you pretend to be very hungry and thirsty. Ask her to give you some make-believe nourishment like leaf lemonade and a grass sandwich on a pretend plate. What will your child do with you? How your child relates to you, the one needing help, will be a good indication as to how he will relate to needy people. Whether the response is positive or negative, you have created a make-believe dramatic episode from which parental instruction and training can be given. Jesus' profound message, "I was hungry and you gave Me food. . . . Inasmuch as you did it to one of the least of these My brethren, you did it to Me" (Matt. 25:35, 40), can be etched on his conscience.

A life-sustaining message of showing concern for others is being brought to life by a make-believe game. You, the adult, help the child internalize this message by pretending to be in need.

Sagas Helping Your Child Identify with You

Sprinkler Splash

Is your young son playing in the sprinkler? Why not pull off your shoes and dance fully dressed in the cool water with him? Why not say, "Oh, no! The flood is rising!" as you turn on the garden hose and thoroughly soak him and you with cool blasts of water?

The little son is captured by your playfulness to want to be a little more like you when he grows up.

The Three Little Pigs

Will you bring to life the three little pigs storybook and make it a delightful memory for your daughter? Will you nestle her snugly in your lap, open the book, and begin reading in a high, squealing voice, "Once upon a time, three little pigs went out in the world to seek their fortune"? Will you "huff and puff and blooow their houses down" in a deep, gruff voice as the big, bad wolf?

The little daughter feels close because you took five minutes out of your busy schedule to be playfully creative with her.

A Saga Teaching Good Work Ethics

Suppose your young child is being lazy. He has difficulty doing a good job of even a simple work task. How do you help him take responsibility and pride in a job well done? Do you know how to make fun out of work?

"Oh, dear! This floor is a mess! Look at all those scuffs and crumbs! We'll just have to clean the kitchen tile right away!" exclaims the mother as she studies the marks and stains on her linoleum floor. "We'll just have to skate away all that ugly mess!" she concludes with a nod. Sitting down on the floor, she ties an old washcloth with a string around each of her bare feet, stands up, and cautiously tests her homemade skates.

She has conveniently made all her ice-skating preparations in front of her young child. Doing all her actions with pretended deep concentration, she suddenly looks up with surprise, as if struck with a thought: "Jon, would you like to ice-skate, too?"

More than likely, Jon will be fascinated with the idea of ice-skating on the kitchen floor. Naturally, his skates are ready and waiting for him on the counter. After tying old washcloths on his bare feet, the mother pours warm sudsy water on the linoleum tile and begins to move with slow skating motion around the kitchen. She strides, makes circles, weaves backward, and thoroughly scrubs clean her sticky kitchen floor, along with little Jon's enthusiastic help.

A good saga in a companionship game is the creative tale being told, the make-believe yarn being spun, the dramatic action being played out, and the deeper message you are attempting to convey. That message may be as simple as "Let's have some nonsensical fun!" to as basic as "Work is good and can be enjoyed" to as profound a spiritual truth as Jesus' words: "I was hungry and you gave Me food."

The dramatic episode in companionship games enables you to connect with your child and pass on life-sustaining messages to your child's heart. Basically, there are two types of companionship games which accomplish this. Both combine drama and storytelling in creative make-believe games of endearment and games of adventure.

Creative companionship games of endearment and adventure are designed to be captivating sagas with delightful dramatic episodes that spellbind a child. Make-believe activities are brought to life, and you and your child are brought closer together.

Basically, there are two types of sagas: the saga of endearment and the saga of adventure. Both combine the telling of a story and the acting out of an activity.

The Saga of Endearment

A saga of endearment allows the adult to begin playing on a very elementary level. Let's examine a saga of endearment and see what it weaves.

The father settles Josh in his lap and gently pats his chubby legs. Clearing his throat, the father speaks almost in a whisper, "The itsy, bitsy spider climbed up the water spout. Down came the rain and washed the spider out. Up popped the sun and dried up all the rain. And the itsy, bitsy spider climbed up the spout again."

This beloved nursery rhyme has doubtlessly been spoken, sung, or acted out for generations. The rhyme is brought to life by the one saying it. Usually, the speaker's hand is the spider, the child's leg or arm is the spout, and the itsy, bitsy spider hand tickles a passageway up the child's wiggly, giggly body.

There is no involved story or intricate imagery in the saga of endearment. Rather, the story line is simple, and the fantasy is uncomplicated. The single plot activity may be communicated in a quiet, slow-moving pace or as simple action. The parent and the child share a moment of friendship.

Weaving a saga of endearment means that an imaginary play-ful activity is verbally spoken and is creatively brought to life by the speaker. This is done in quiet, nonthreatening ways; one whispers a secret or shows hidden treasure in his hand to a best friend. Or it may be in a more active way; one tickles a playmate for fun.

The Saga of Adventure

A saga of adventure allows the adult to expand his creative and imaginative abilities to a higher level. A saga of adventure al-lows the adult to weave a sense of oneness by using more action and intrigue.

Floating in the swimming pool, the nine-year-old daughter is enjoying sliding on and off her raft as her mother dives into the water for a swim. Surfacing with a burst, the mother pre-tends to be a friendly, talking dolphin.

"Hi, there! My name's Spunky. What's your name, little human?" she quizzes. "I love to pull rafts around the pool. Want a ride?" she playfully asks and then dips under the water's surface.

149

This simple invitation introducing a companionship game will likely engage the mother and child in a laughing, splashing fun time. The action and story line may become quite involved; surprise and intrigue may lace the activities invented by both parent and child; creative inspiration may trigger the daughter's imagination, and she becomes a talking dolphin, too.

The itsy bitsy spider companionship game illustrates a saga of endearment and the talking dolphin companionship game illustrates a saga of adventure. Let's look closer at the elements that make up the two types of sagas and that make each distinct.

How Sagas of Endearment and Adventure Are Alike

Both Use Imaginary Activity

Remember, a unique feature of all make-believe companionship games is imaginary activity. How this imaginary activity is carried out usually indicates whether the companionship game is a saga of endearment or a saga of adventure. Younger and older children may thoroughly enjoy both types of companionship games.

Sagas of endearment are easy first-step approaches to engaging in creative play. They build the bridges of communication for future, more involved creative play.

Being more advanced in creative make-believe does not mean that sagas of adventure are better than sagas of endearment. Rather, they usually are more intricate and appealing to an older child whose mind and creativity are more developed. Like a saga of endearment, a saga of adventure uses imaginary and real activity to invent a story. Also, the sense of oneness between the parent and the child is predominantly conveyed through the activity. A saga of adventure maximizes actions and words to visualize the fantasy for the child; it may use many layers of events upon which to build a companionship game.

In a saga of endearment, imagery is used, but a sense of oneness is communicated with fewer words and less action. These sagas are ideal for small children, who have difficulty in speaking or engaging in intricate activities. A single event is capitalized on, and oneness is woven around that event.

Both Bring Inanimate Objects to Life

A saga of endearment focuses more on inanimate objects coming to life than a saga of adventure does. Since the imaginary activity usually centers on fewer objects, it is important to give these objects motion and life to keep interest. Something unusual should be woven into the activity. One of the easiest ways to bring an object to life is to give it thoughts, feelings, or actions similar to one's personality.

A saga of adventure also uses inanimate objects in a creative manner but brings these objects to life in a general sense. There is less concentration on the specific object and more concentration on the activity. The object's presence adds to the story rather than its being the story around which the activity is centered.

How Sagas of Endearment and Adventure Differ

Singling Out with Pet Names or Terms

Sagas of endearment give special attention to the child rather than focus on a fun activity with the child. Sagas of adventure tend more to blend that focus, with the activity playing a larger role.

In a saga of endearment, the adult singles out one particular child and communicates how wonderfully special and beloved the child is in the adult's life. Since a saga of endearment tends to focus exclusively on one child at a time, it is vital that parents give equal time to all children. Every child in a family should experience a saga of endearment with each parent—at different times, of course.

The adult accomplishes this special feeling by inventing pet names or terms for the object, the child, or both. These names or terms are never to be embarrassing or humiliating to the child. They are never to be immodest or crude in regard to the object. Usually, a body part is selected as the beloved object; appropriate body parts are fingers, hands, feet, and toes. Other favorite things, such as a teddy bear, doll, or blanket, may be used. The object is given an identity and personality.

If the child is given a pet name or term, the adult must be certain that the child regards that name or term as endearing and special. One of the quickest ways to alienate a child in a relationship is to label that child with a despised nickname. In fact, endearing terms are to be private within the household; they are not for public hearing. They are never to replace the child's real name.

What endearing terms am I talking about? The terms should be characteristic of and in keeping with the spirit of a saga of endearment companionship game. Since companionship games are to be creative, fun, and playful expressions of a person's child-like qualities, so the endearing terms should be creative, fun, and playful expressions of a person's unique and delightful personality. Since sagas of endearment may be nonsensical, with catchy phrases and humor, endearing terms should be expressed in the same manner.

Terms are to be pleasant, descriptive, endearing comments about a child or an object. There may be a rascally element to the term, but it's never hurtful or critical. A mother may lovingly comment, "Is my pet dragon awake yet?" as she stirs her sleepy nine-year-old son out of bed. Knowing that he is a little grumpy in the morning, she is playfully nudging him toward getting up by using an endearing, though rascally, term.

If the son says, "Awww, Mom, don't call me that!" he indicates that he does not like the term, and the adult should stop using it immediately. However, he might peek open one eye, give a muffled gruff at being awakened and a slight smile at the affectionate term his mom just called him: "Yeah, it's kinda like me."

Such a term as "pet dragon" lovingly spoken by a parent would qualify as a term of endearment only if the child responded positively.

Varied Degrees of Adventure

In companionship games, both the saga of endearment and the saga of adventure have an element of high adventure. There is to be an element of drama, suspense, or mystery, which adds to the sense that the child and the adult are having a marvelous, exciting adventure of some sort.

However, the saga of endearment does not involve the dramatic and mysterious to as intense a degree as does the saga of adventure. Generally, its quieter, calmer motion or simpler story line does not lend itself to developing an intricate exploit. Snuggling in Daddy's lap, feeling safe and secure while acting out a nonsensical nursery rhyme or bringing to life a beloved storybook, is a wonderful moment of bonding. The adventure is relatively predictable due to the built-in repetition in the game.

Creative repetition is good. Children need creative fun that is predictable and familiar. Children can listen with raptured silence to a beloved fairy tale being retold or reread for the hundredth time.

Though drama occurs in sagas of endearment, it is more readily experienced in sagas of adventure. The story line is involved and the movement more active; the drama and suspense can quickly build up and produce intrigue.

Because drama is built into sagas of adventure, you should use them with discernment. Is the activity going to precede a restful time? Downplay or minimize the dramatic element to some degree or situate it early within the activity so that the child can be more smoothly introduced to a nap at the conclusion of the activity. Is the saga of adventure occurring during an active period of the child's day? Let the dramatic element be wholeheartedly expressed, and enjoy a romping make-believe adventure with your youngster.

Companionship games enable you to dramatically communicate all sorts of episodes and profoundly affect your child with life-sustaining messages. Creative games of endearment and adventure are designed to connect you to your child in a dramatic and fun way. Imaginative games can capture your child's heart and win him over to listen to and receive all the heart messages you deeply desire to communicate to him.

Some Parents Face Something Bigger

Companionship games help to creatively unite parent and child in a fun and meaningful make-believe activity. Some parents dearly wish needing to get better acquainted and bonded with their children was the biggest hurdle in the relationship. Instead, they are at war with their youngsters and feel that they are losing the battle.

How can the power struggle between parent and child be

constructively defused so that both feel more bonded? Can the struggle ever be won and the child and the adult feel a heart closeness? Yes! It can be done!

Let's discover some creative secrets of positively engaging in this relational war and how the parent can win the child's heart in a more loving relationship. Let's explore some unique ways to get the child to forgo animosity and become a best friend.

CHAPTER 11

Creative Opposite Games of Make-Believe

"Deborah, it's still there! Your belly button is still right on your tummy! Tonight I'm going to rub it off! Hold very still. No wiggling or giggling! I have to erase it!" exclaims the mother, pretending to be surprised that her child's tiny belly button is still right where it has been for the last six years of Deborah's life.

The mother begins to tickle the hard-to-remove spot, still with no success. "Deborah, it won't come off! I can't erase it. You stop laughing this minute! I'm trying my best to remove it!" states the mother with feigned exasperation at her daughter's giggly behavior over such a serious situation.

The little daughter's wiggling and laughing trigger another playful round of tickling as the mother pretends to become more frustrated. "No, you can't get my belly button, Mommy! You can't have it!" breathlessly squeals the little girl.

"What am I going to do with you? I want that belly button now! Give it to me right this minute!" playfully demands the mother as she pretends to be exhausted with the rubbing.

"No! No! No! You can't have it!" laughs Deborah as her mother finally stops tickling her tummy and pretends to look disappointed and sad.

"I didn't get it off tonight, but I'm going to tomorrow! You wait and see," concludes the mother.

What is going on? This creative opposite game has great prospects of defusing the real-life power struggle between Jessica and her mother. That is what is occurring as the adult and the child creatively play together.

How can such an interaction defuse anything, much less the animosity between a child and a parent? Let's look closely at an opposite game and how it does just that.

What Is an Opposite Game?

Opposite games are the second major category of creative play that profoundly touches the heart of a child. Whereas companionship games blend the parent and the child together as best friends on the same team, opposite games playfully pit the adult and the child as competitors in a mock battle or contest. However, in this contest the adult purposefully comes out the loser.

The same loving attitudes, dramatic action, and good episodes of companionship games apply to opposite games. The fun and relational elements of best friends remain the same between parent and child. The difference lies in the intent behind opposite games. Companionship games have the intent of good friends playfully sharing a team spirit together in an activity or adventure; opposite games have the intent of good friends pretending mock rivalry in a contest where the adult loses.

Before looking at why this intent is central in defusing the power struggle between parent and child, you must understand the makeup of an opposite game.

Similarities Between Opposite and Companionship Games

Both Involve Make-Believe

Both opposite and companionship games involve imaginative activity. In both, the participants pretend someone or something is other than what it really is.

In companionship games, the movement and story are developed along a realistic line. When fantasy occurs, objects and people generally follow a believable story line rather than behave out of character for what is being imagined.

In opposite games, objects and people are imagined other than what they are; however, there is an even greater, rascally opposite touch to their imagined behavior. There is a mischievous twist to or playful and unexpected reversal of the story line. This reversal is more than a mock mishap in a companionship game, which adds a touch of real-life drama to the game.

An opposite game stages a make-believe reversal of the normal or expected as a central part of the game. The mother trying to erase her daughter's belly button is a good example. The entire focus of the game is on an adult's imagined attempts at accomplishing something impossible to do. The playful twist or reverse is that the adult places herself in an opposite position from her normal role of being in charge.

Both Are Sagas of Endearment or Adventure

Opposite games, like companionship games, are designed to spellbind the child in a saga of endearment or adventure. The elements that make up a good saga are the same for both. There is to be a blending of real and make-believe; games are to have a beginning, a playtime, and an ending. There is a dramatic episode played out, and underlying heart messages are conveyed to the child.

As in a companionship game, the saga of endearment in an opposite game is focused more on the child than on the activity. In fact, an opposite game lends itself to almost exclusive focus on the child and very little emphasis on an involved story line or adventure. The belly button eraser opposite game beginning this chapter involves only the mother, the child, and the child's belly button. The simplicity of opposite games almost resembles the simplicity of the sagas of endearment in companionship games.

There is considerable active movement but not the dramatic touches of real or pretend props or an intriguing story line usually found in companionship sagas of adventure. Basically, the motion in opposite game sagas most resembles the level of motion in companionship sagas of adventure. For instance, the river rapid companionship game in chapter 10 was filled with physical action. The refrigerator box boat swirled and rocked over the churning mountain river; the child was playfully bounced and tumbled; there was a lot of giggling, laughter, and body movement.

Opposite games focus on the child while being highly active in body motion and highly expressive in body language. The belly button eraser opposite game has the potential of becoming a wiggling, giggling, tickling match between mother and child with both quickly getting out of breath.

An opposite game may be scaled down to a simple one-liner contest and even use terms of endearment in a calm manner to spellbind the child. As a saga of endearment, an opposite game may be played more quietly and with less body movement than a companionship game.

Both Use the Teaming-Up Concept

Both companionship games and opposite games are playful concoctions of the imagination in which the team concept is used. The former uses the team concept as companions against an imaginary opponent. The latter uses this concept as team competitors playfully pitting themselves against each other.

Goodwill and fair play are equally involved in both types of games. Only love, friendship, and acceptance are to be communicated between participants in the make-believe games. A healthy team spirit is to be experienced, whether the creative play is a companionship or an opposite game.

Recognizing the general similarities between companionship games and opposite games will help you more fully understand the differences. Both are creative play; both accomplish more loving ties between parent and child; both do so in different ways.

Let's look closely at the three unique parts of an opposite game. The differences from a companionship game make it ideal as a creative means to defuse power struggles between parent and child.

Three Distinct Elements of Opposite Games

Opposite games consist of three basic elements that are blended together to spellbind a youngster: (1) they are mock contests where (2) parent and child are friendly antagonists and (3) the adult loses the contest. You must understand the makeup of an opposite game if you want to creatively use it to build emotional bonds with your child.

Element #1:
The Adult Stages a Mock Contest

In an opposite game, you think up a fun-filled activity or event that would appeal to the age and disposition of your child. It may be nonsensical, like the belly button eraser game, or it may be more thought provoking.

Either way, the child must perceive it as a contest. Winning in a vague manner will not amount to much in the child's estimation. Rather, the child is facing an exciting challenge! You can effectively fuel this perception in a number of ways.

You convey this idea by reversing what is expected. If the contest is nonsensical, you pretend that the activity is vitally important and you must win it. If the contest is a genuine, challenging activity, you create something opposite from the normal within the game to add a touch of teasing competition. Let's look at the belly button eraser game and then the whying opposite game to see how this works.

A Nonsensical Mock Contest

In the belly button eraser opposite game, the mother picked a playful, tickling activity with which to engage her six-year-old daughter. The adult made it into a contest by pretending that the child's belly button had to be removed.

In fact, removing Deborah's belly button became a vitally important task in the game. The mock contest was staged as the mother made a determined but impossible attempt to erase it.

The child experienced a nonsensical, gleeful activity made into a competition by the mother's reversing the normal. Belly buttons are supposed to stay on tummies.

Nonsensical mock contests allow the child to successfully compete against the adult just for fun. The profound defusing effect of this will be discussed later.

A Serious Mock Contest

Opposite games are playful contests that may also have a serious tone. You may wish to express something other than just fun. You may wish to teach an important lesson or share a truth that affects your child's heart. You stage a mock contest that is the reverse of what the child normally experiences; it catches the child's undivided attention by its opposite nature. The whying game is a good example.

"*Why* are white shiny lines painted in the middle of the highway?" asks the father driving his family on summer vacation. His four-year-old twin sons look curiously out the van window at the dividing lines flashing past them down the road.

"I don't know," one son wonders out loud.

"They look pretty!" offers the other.

"They are pretty, but *why* would someone paint pretty white lines down the middle of the highway?" continues Dad.

"The paint keeps cars where they belong!" thoughtfully responds one child.

"Yes! But *why* do cars need to stay where they belong?" counters the father. "*Why* should our car stay on this side of the road and that blue car stay on the other side?"

"Daddy! You know, so the cars won't hit each other!" squeal both boys as if in mental competition with their father.

"But *why* would it be bad if our cars hit each other?" continues the father as he poses one *why* question after another while driving down the highway.

The whying opposite game sets thought-provoking questions before a child in the context of a game. Normally, the child peppers the adult with endless questions about life and the world. In the whying game, the adult bombards the child with interesting questions one after the other until the child finally tires and asks the adult to stop talking so *he* can rest for a while.

Element #2:
The Adult Is a Playful Antagonist

As a playful antagonist, you reverse the normal role of caregiver and nurturer. You become a playful competitor to prompt your child to want to win.

Your intentions, words, and actions are to be gentle and good-humored. However, you make the challenge in all seriousness and with a touch of parental authority.

As a playful antagonist, remember that your size, skill, strength, and intellect are of no consequence. Make believe that the contestants are equally matched or that your child has the competitive edge.

Element #3:
The Adult Loses

In opposite games, you as the big friendly antagonist challenge your child in a contest that you lose. Your defeat is the main feature that allows opposite games to defuse the real-life power struggles between you and your child.

You fuel the perception of losing a contest in a number of ways: You assume the role of defeated opponent, you allow your child to savor victories, and you reissue the challenge in the future.

The Adult Is a Good Make-Believe Loser

You position yourself to lose the make-believe contest. Opposite games allow your child to primarily win and you to primarily lose. This outcome is a reverse of real-life competition between parent and child. It also reverses the usual idea of losing. In opposite games, it is just as much fun to lose as to win.

The staged throw is a unique feature of opposite games. You manufacture a win for your child in the make-believe play. Words and actions are the challenge designed to involve the child in the activity.

In the belly button eraser game, the mother challenged her child with verbal commands: "No wiggling or giggling! Be still!" She boasted, "This time I'm going to rub it off!" and pretended she would succeed in removing the belly button. Through comments that challenge, the adult created an atmosphere for the staged throw.

Sometimes the child refuses to make a winning throw, and the adult may need to coach. A child who is in emotional trench warfare with the parent may totally refuse to budge, even in a creatively playful direction. The real-life problem must be addressed before make-believe games will improve the relationship.

A child may be shy or afraid to participate in opposite games for less drastic reasons. The adult is being an approachable, friendly authority figure, and the child is not used to it. A pleasant prod or incentive added to the win may coax the child to make the winning throw. For instance, Deborah's mother could say, "Deborah, if I don't get your belly button off after school tomorrow, I'll bake your favorite chocolate cake! That will teach you!"

The Adult Allows the Child to Savor the Victory

You affectionately enter the revelry of your child's victory. Before the winning throw, you may say, "I give up! I give up! You're the winner, Champ!" After the throw, you exclaim, "You beat me, you little rascal! I'll get you next time!"

Allow your child to savor the triumph over you. Good-naturedly endure your child's announcement: "I'm the winner!"

We Will Resume This Challenge

The final touch is the future challenge that rises from the defeated parent. "I will try again!" or "I will return!" is a verbal affirmation that you will engage your child in a future contest. The idea that more contests are to come signals your future playful involvement with your child. Your child will remind you to creatively play, knowing full well he will playfully trounce his friendly antagonist just one more time.

The three basic elements provide the structure upon which the opposite feature is built. Opposite games are layered with features that add a playful twist to reality. This imaginative reverse of the normal or expected sets the stage for the high-spirited interaction that develops through the game. Understanding the opposite feature will help you skillfully use it in defusing the real-life power struggles you face in parenting.

The Opposite Intent

The underlying feature of opposite games is an unusual, outrageous, or impossible intent on the part of the parent. In the belly button eraser game, this key element occurs again and again. The parent is shocked that the child's tiny belly button is still on her tummy. The impossible intent is seen when the parent tries desperately to erase it and fails. Belly buttons do not disappear when they are rubbed!

These playful reversals form the basis for the mock situation. There is no real problem, only a nonsensical, make-believe one. The parent is building a mock problem or contest for the purpose of allowing the child to win in a playful and creative way.

Laughter, playful teasing, good interaction, and wholesome parental contact and attention may be experienced in an opposite game. These reasons alone improve a relationship.

However, grasping the deeper impact of opposite games and skillfully using them to defuse power struggles are far more important. Communicating heart messages through reversing the expected is a profound way in which to speak to your child and may be significantly accomplished through a creative opposite game.

Five Profound Factors of Opposite Games

Let's examine the impact and importance of you becoming a playful antagonist who loses in a mock contest with your child. Good opposite games may reverse power struggles and allow the parent and child to become best friends. How and why does the imaginative and playful reversal reduce tension? Five profound factors behind opposite games are responsible for improving the communication and interaction. Let's closely examine an opposite game and find out.

Tickle Me to Sleep Opposite Game

"Now, Carl, Daddy wants you to be real quiet and go to sleep! Absolutely, positively, without a shadow of a doubt, no playing around! No wiggling, giggling, laughing, bouncing, or squealing! I want you to be a good, quiet little boy for the rest of the night! I'm going to pull up the sheets and tuck them in all snug under your chin. Shhh! Now, close your eyes and lie real still," directs the young father putting his four-year-old to bed.

The overly serious, yet playful, enunciation of every word, the teasing animation in his voice, the preoccupation with the sheets, the smile on his face, and the twinkle in his eyes signal a playful twist to the father's words. A wonderful opposite game is about to begin in which the father has playfully positioned himself as a friendly antagonist about to lose a make-believe contest.

Just as Carl squeezes tight his eyes and lies still to comply with his father's request, his dad suddenly tickles his sides through the sheets. Squirming, laughing, and squealing with de-light, the young son absolutely, positively, without a shadow of a doubt cannot lie still and quiet like a good little boy going to sleep.

Carl's dad may cry out in feigned shock and disbelief over his son's disobedient and romping behavior: "Carl, I told you to be still! Stop laughing this very minute! Stop wiggling so much!" Then he continues tickling his little son, making it im-possible for the child to comply.

The weary father finally gives up in mock frustration and defeat: "Carl, I don't know what I'm going to do with you." Then in mock resignation he drops his shaking head, slumps his broad shoulders, and lets his hands hang down at his side.

The child's likely response to this romping opposite game? "Daddy! Daddy! Do it again! Please!"

What profound factors occur in an opposite game?

Factor #1:
Shared Authority

In the tickle-me-to-sleep game, Carl decides the outcome, and the father submits to his decision. Granted, Carl can't help making the decision to continue laughing, and the father has shared decision-making authority by playfully constructing a winning situation for his son.

By creatively constructing an opposite game, you allow your child to have authority over you in the context of a make-believe game. You are not really abdicating your proper and rightful position of leadership. You are not inappropriately submitting to a child in real life. Only in play are you allowing your child to have authority.

How does your child exercise this authority over you? Your child experiences make-believe authority by playfully defying your unusual, outrageous, or impossible request. Why allow a child authority in the first place, even in play? All children secretly long to be in charge over parents and tell them what they can and cannot do, just like parents tell them.

In reality, allowing the child to have command of the relationship would be unhealthy and even detrimental. However, when the parent willingly shares authority with the child by allowing her to rule and win in a make-believe game, the real-life power struggle is defused. The child is totally in charge of the situation; the adult is totally under the child's command in a creative opposite game.

Some of the very real desire to be in charge is defused in a romping, playful way. The real-life struggle to be in charge is vicariously met by being in charge in creative make-believe play.

Factor #2:
Felt Sense of Fair Play

Carl's feelings of being fairly treated are heightened as his father pretends varied levels of frustration and tries different solutions to the situation. The child experiences winning one moment and possibly losing the next as the tickling game continues.

When you share authority with your child in a game, the child usually experiences an inner sense of being fairly treated. You are giving authority as well as taking authority in the relationship. In real life, a child often perceives an adult as only taking authority; the relationship seems one-sided and unfair. In an opposite game, your child experiences a two-sided arrangement in the relationship when you playfully share authority; the child perceives that you are being fair. Granted, it is only in play, yet your child will likely emotionally tally up fairness on your ledger of interaction.

In effect, you honor your child's innate sense that there should be an equal give-and-take in best friend relationships. The child unrealistically and erroneously supposes that this equal give-and-take should occur in everything. You creatively meet a very real emotional need within your child when you playfully share authority with him.

Because authority is the last area where you are apt to share with your child, opposite games facilitate a healthy exchange. Opposite games allow you to playfully give authority to your child so that she does not feel that she must aggressively take authority into her own hands. Opposite games reduce your child's felt sense that you are taking unfair advantage of her and not behaving as a best friend who shares. Most children believe that their parents always get to have the final word on everything. In an opposite game, your child has the authoritative last say in a wholesome make-believe adventure.

Factor #3:
Identifying Through Role Reversal

The father is being a playful prankster with his young son. The lighthearted manner of the dad identifies him as a fun-loving, youthful good friend. The adult's normal leadership role is momentarily switched for a less parental one.

Have you ever wanted to be deeply understood by another? Have you ever wished that the person you loved dearly could get inside your skin and feel, think, and see things from your perspective? Your child deeply longs for the most significant adult in his life—his parent—to look at him with more identity and more understanding of his childlike qualities.

In an opposite game, you purposefully switch roles with your child to promote that identity. The child becomes the leader and you become the follower in a variety of ways and at numerous levels.

The dramatized action and animated behavior identify you with your child. A child thinks and acts in terms of bigger than life and out of the ordinary. When you creatively behave in these ways, your child perceives that you know and understand how a youngster thinks, feels, and acts.

The novel idea of switching places with you is spellbinding in itself. What child does not dream of what she will do and how she will act when she is grown up? And right now, she is being allowed to appropriately act out this fantasy in an opposite game.

Does role reversal confuse a child with an unhealthy flight into fantasy? If the child knows that the behavior is only a part of a make-believe game being creatively played for a short period of time before returning to reality, he will accept it for what it is: a delightful moment that wonderfully touches his heart to feel closer to you.

In an opposite game, you lovingly identify with your child— even up to impersonating her—to be like her for a few brief, unforgettable moments. You do this to help your child perceive you as one who understands and who is trying to playfully meet some of her secret longings by getting into her skin in a creative way.

Factor #4:
Emotional Safety Release Valve

Carl is able to squeal, "No! No! No!" at his father's requests to stop laughing and wiggling. He is allowed to disregard all the adult's requests to be still, quiet, and go to sleep. The child will likely become exhausted with all the squirming and out of breath with all the laughter.

Many opposite games are designed to be emotional safety release valves for the real-life negative pressure that often builds up in a relationship. Opposite games are preventive activities in that they often help the adult bypass much of the negative power struggle that would otherwise occur in a relationship. They are even remedial activities in the sense of helping to restore a hurting or broken relationship. However, whether preventive or remedial, they are not to be used to superficially let off steam, get revenge, get even, or score an underhanded point in a pretentious way. Most children will be quick to perceive such intent by parents, which will effectively destroy any positive bonding that might otherwise have happened. An emotional safety release

171

valve refers to the built-in defusing characteristic of opposite games when properly played. It works like this.

The parent whose interaction with the child predominantly focuses on correcting, instructing, and disciplining the child is most likely headed for a power struggle. The child longs to shout a resounding, emphatic, "No! I won't comply! I won't do what you want or say!" in the face of the parent. Often, that is exactly what a strong-willed child or older child will do. Of course, in real life, the parent should correct such a rebellious response. And many power struggles result even when the parents mix proper discipline with interaction with the children.

Allowing a playful, energetic "no" response in a game is a positive, almost pleasant counterresponse. It is not a disrespectful, negative, or truly hostile reaction that is being permitted.

What if you skillfully construct a make-believe contest in which you encourage your child to playfully counter you? In many opposite games, that is exactly what occurs. Because the desire or action is playfully ludicrous or impossible to obey, your child experiences in harmless play what is properly forbidden in real life.

The overall effect of an opposite game provides an emotional safety release valve for the child. It provides an appropriate, legitimate occasion to say a playful but firm no to the parent, which is acceptable because it is said in the context of a make-believe game.

Factor #5:
Endearment Leading to Emulation

Carl's daddy is playing with him in a fun-filled way. He is holding, hugging, laughing, and tickling his little son in a nonsensical game of make-believe. "Daddy! Daddy, do it again!" is the child's declaration that he not only identifies with and loves the father's attention and the activity but that he will likely want to copy both.

The fifth factor—endearment leading to emulation—lies at the heart of why these make-believe activities so profoundly communicate to a child. Combining the first four factors helps to communicate your underlying endearment and love toward your child despite struggles and differences. Opposite games provide the invaluable avenue for the message of love and endearment to get through the maze of differences and power struggles that naturally occur between parent and child.

As your love and endearment are conveyed to the receptive heart of your child through the creative play of opposite games, many times a wonderful transformation occurs in the child. The child's receptivity to you as the authority increases, as does her receptivity to your ways of thinking. Your child may want to be more like you and may take on your values as her own.

The fifth factor involves your tremendous ability to influence your child. It stirs your child to want to emulate you because you have lovingly endeared yourself to the child through creative play.

This transformation of heart may be gradual or sudden; it may occur to a greater or lesser degree in different children, but it generally occurs. Why? The heart reasoning of a child is, *I will listen to the one who understands and loves me.* The one a person listens to with his heart is the one he becomes like and whose values he assumes as his own.

Let's see how endearment leading to emulation works. The "I love you! I said it first! I win!" game is an excellent example of reversing the expected and winning a child's heart in the process.

The mother tiptoes up to her son and says, "I love you! I said it first! I win, Jonathan!"

Her young son may respond in several ways. He may look at her with surprise and confusion and say nothing. He may smile and respond, "I love you, too." He may shrug a reply or make a negative or sarcastic comment.

The child's response is not the parent's focus. The mother stays in character as mischief maker and counters, "Well, I do love you, and I did say it first. So I win! Maybe you'll win next time if you're quick." The mother then casually walks off as if nothing unusual happened, leaving her son to ponder the out-of-the-ordinary action and comment.

The mother may repeat this loving challenge several times that day or through the week. She is truly sincere, yet there is a rascally intonation in her voice. The child knows she is serious and teasing at the same time.

The child's natural curiosity will eventually peak, or he will be playfully challenged once too often. "I love you, and I said it first! So there! Now I win!" he finally responds.

"No! Oh, no! You beat me!" reacts the startled mother. "You said it first! How could this happen?" She may stagger backward as if pretending to be overwhelmed by the reality of losing the contest.

The child inwardly likes winning over his parent. He may give himself an emotional pat on the back for outwitting his mom—even if it was just a silly challenge she was making.

The mother continues in character a moment longer. Shaking her head in mock disbelief, she behaves with stunned amazement at actually losing the contest. Pretending to be unable to grasp the situation, she mutters to herself, "I lost. I actually lost!" and slowly walks to the kitchen to begin supper.

However, just before entering the kitchen, she turns with re-newed determination in her voice: "OK! OK! Jonathan you may have won this time, but I won't lose tomorrow!"

Opposite games may have much intrigue, or they may be less-dramatic creative inventions of the imagination. Opposite games may be crammed full of words and actions, or they may be quieter-word-and-slower-action dialogues that reduce hostili-ties in a creative way.

However they are played, the central theme of expressing love and endearment by the reverse technique is identifiably present. The purpose of a make-believe reversal is to unleash the five factors in real life. Let's look closely at the "I love you!" opposite game and see how the five factors were creatively played out and what was really communicated.

A Closer Look

In this briefly worded game, all five factors are present to some degree. That is excellent; however, it is not necessarily bet-ter to have all factors present to play an opposite game.

Factors #1, #2, and #3 are present in a general sense. The mother shares authority by coaxing the child to win over her, which puts the grown-up in submission as a defeated contestant. The adult does this in a fair give-and-take manner. "I win this time; you win next time if you want" is her playful invitation, even though her words are couched in a creative challenge. The role reversal factor is possibly the least obvious. Actually, the adult initially clamors to be first at something in the relationship. Young children naturally race to get ahead, be first, or get the most in a competition. The adult's saying, "I can beat you," and acting like a teasing prankster are two other noticeable role re-versals.

In this opposite game, factor #4 and factor #5 are blended; they are the truly significant influences in defusing the power struggle.

Are you able to pick up on factor #4, an emotional release occurring in this opposite game? There is a wonderful emotional release in finally being allowed to compete to get ahead of another in a relationship. It helps to defuse the power struggle between parent and child by creatively saying, "Yes!" in make-believe to what is usually forbidden in real life.

The winning that occurs is only a mock battle and victory played in a creative make-believe game and not in a real-life situation. It is a positive encounter in which the child is allowed to playfully counter authority and win in some way. There is never to be truly hostile, prideful, or hurtful competition between adult and child.

By engaging in the mock contest, what good attitude was the child coaxed to copy? In this opposite game, what qualities expressed by the adult was the child encouraged to emulate?

This brings us to factor #5, the central intent of all opposite games: the child's emulation of good values because his heart was captured by a playful reversal.

The child struggled, strived, and playfully fought to be first in this make-believe opposite game. He was lovingly prodded by the adult to compete and win the contest. Defeating his parental authority figure was good and praiseworthy because by winning and being the first to say, "I love you!" he expressed a sentiment that most parents desperately want their children to feel and willingly express.

The heart message of "I love you" is given an avenue of expression that is sincere and nonthreatening for people who have difficulty communicating their feelings. For people who find it easy to express endearing terms, this game allows them to do so even more readily. Participants get in the habit of saying, "I love you," to each other. What is repeated and becomes comfortable in a game is said more often and becomes more meaningful in real life.

This make-believe opposite game allows parent and child to coach each other in becoming comfortable and familiar with saying and meaning loving terms of endearment. Showing verbal endearment is fun and meaningful.

In good opposite games, the five factors may blend in various ways to reduce the real-life power struggle in a family. The overall defusing effect occurs as the child experiences playful victory over the parental authority figure in these creative, unexpected ways. And the mock victories are surrounded by the parent's loving and endearing behavior.

Heart Connection by Reversing the Expected

Why does a creative reversal of the normal and expected have such a captivating effect on a child's attention and affection? This is a legitimate question, and there may not be an easy answer. However, one thing evident from Scripture is that the Lord Jesus used the relational technique of reversing the expected to spellbind His listeners and speak to their hearts.

The story of the prodigal son showed the father welcoming back his wayward and disobedient child with open arms and loving actions, even celebrating the son's return with a party. How unexpected after the son caused such grief and loss! Welcoming him home as a beloved son to be honored reversed what he and his older brother expected. (See Luke 15.) The father's love was profoundly demonstrated to both by a creative opposite.

Perhaps that is the key—creatively, lovingly reversing the normal has a way of getting the attention of one's listeners and helping them hear the truth being communicated. The normal way of thinking and doing something may not necessarily be the most effective (or the most right and loving) way of communicating a message.

Reversing the expected often has a way of cutting through barriers and communicating truth straight to the heart. Creative play in an opposite game has somewhat the same effect. Normally, it is thought that only youngsters are supposed to play make-believe games. Mature adults have long ago outgrown such activities. Mature people are in full authority and control of themselves, their families, and their situations.

Such reasoning causes the adult to suppose her child will regard and listen to her better when relating in this mature way. The adult may believe that being childlike is foolish or that identifying with her youngster in a playfully creative manner is unimportant.

In reality, when you become playfully childlike, your child regards you with greater and truer respect and authority. Your obedience to Christ's command to "become like a child" is practically worked out in your relationship with your child. Also, you are demonstrating the same spiritual qualities that your child naturally possesses. Becoming creatively playful allows you to relationally identify with your audience, much like the apostle Paul identified with his (1 Cor. 9:19–22). As you blend the physical and the spiritual qualities of a child, life-giving messages are heard and received by your child as relational barriers are removed. By becoming childlike, you more greatly influence your child to become mature and put away childish behavior—quite the opposite of what most adults expect! The more you are playfully childlike and creative, the more likely you will win your youngster's heart.

Of course, the reversal or opposite of what is expected should always be good, right, and truthful in itself. From the perspective of this book, creative play is based on the biblical standard of right and wrong, good and bad; it is an imaginative outworking of the godly qualities of the more excellent way of love (1 Cor. 13).

Opposite games playfully copy the Master's skillful way of communicating truth to the human heart. Through opposite games, you attempt to reach your child's heart. Creative play communicates truth in a language the child knows and easily understands. You are fully capable of mastering this art of communication and connecting with your child's heart for a lifetime.

Now It Is Time to Play

It is time for you to take a journey into the world of creative play! Experience all that has been discussed. Imagine being an invisible guest at a household filled with children where creative play routinely occurs. Witness the fun, the spellbinding, and the messages communicated to youngsters whose ages range from several months to over sixteen years. Join the family and share creative play. Then go and share it with your precious youngster.

Part 4

**Creative Games
for Adult and Child
to Play**

Creative Make-Believe for a Young Child

This chapter introduces a family who creatively plays. All the people are real; all the activities are the make-believe games played over two decades. The family is mine. The creative activities—the adventures shared while the children were young—helped build the emotional bond and unity that grow stronger in their adulthood.

Your circumstances and history may be different; yet much is commonly shared by all family units. Children get up, eat, go to school, come home, and go to bed. Children want parents' time and want them to listen and be there. Children need hugs, love, and the feeling of being bonded with parents. The following creative make-believe games may be used whatever the child's personal circumstances and arrangements may be.

Creative Play for a Very Young Child

The creative play discussed in this chapter applies to a very young child, from a few months to five years of age. Games are not rigidly confined to a child's chronological age. Many make-believe activities span the different age and maturation levels of a child. Continue to play any if wholesome, emotional bonding occurs. Some games you introduce to your very young child may become fond remembrances you share for a lifetime. Never underestimate the profound dynamics of creative play in building and maintaining a healthy, loving relationship.

These examples are just a few of the possible good ways to creatively play with a youngster. You need to imagine, invent, and experiment with your ideas and forms of expression characteristic of your unique personality. Also take into account your child's unique personality when playing. Some games are lively with a romping, rascally quality; others are calm.

Creative games need to communicate your special love and acceptance of your child in a manner characteristic of your unique personality. Though the relational comfort zone may need stretching to include more lively and imaginative interaction, you already are a wonderfully created imagination bearer of God with unique expression. Make-believe games enhance the special person you already are in the eyes of your child. Your child experiences by feeling, seeing, hearing, and touching the love you desire to express.

The following make-believe games take into consideration the very youthfulness of a child from two months to five years of age. In five short years, the child experiences an intense learning process. Time, energy, ability, and interest are focused on the very real task of growing up to a large measure. The child learns to master basic physical and social skills. Add to that the emotional and mental exploration of the world, and you have a very lively, inquisitive, imaginative little human with which to contend.

Learn how to capitalize on your child's activity and exploration. If you truly capture the moment of early childhood, you are much more likely in the process to connect with your child's heart for a lifetime.

Make-Believe Games for the Morning

The focus here is on how to add a touch of creativity and imagination to existing responsibilities. Using make-believe play, learn to get monotonous jobs done more pleasantly, add an exciting spark to the family relationship, and communicate vital messages to the child's heart in the process.

The Big Giant's Tent
Opposite Game of Endearment

The six-year-old and three-year-old peek at their sleeping parents. With a sudden scramble, the three-year-old gleefully hops on the foot of the bed and slowly inches her way through the blankets, close to her parents' faces. "Time to get up, Daddy and Mommy!" she sings. "It's Saturday!" And she playfully pats Daddy's whiskered face and Mommy's tangled hair.

The mother opens her eyes and looks into the face of her little girl and finds it hard to be truly angry. "OK! OK, you! We're awake!" she yawns sleepily and playfully tousles her tangled curls. "Cuddle under the sheets with Daddy and me before you get cold, and try to be still!"

Lifting up the blankets, the mother snuggles her squirmy daughter beside her and lets the bed covering down over both heads. "Now you are in my tent cave! I'm the Big Mommy Giant who lives here! Who are you, little human?" she says.

Then tickling her sides, the mother literally chases her with her fingers under the sheet and down to the bottom of the bed. "And stay there, you squirming human, so I can get some sleep!" she playfully threatens. "And don't tickle my toes!" she adds as she gives her feet a teasing wiggle.

The girl under the blankets at the bottom of the bed naturally finds the Big Giant's toes to tickle, which begins another round of the Giant's frustrated attempt to get sleep.

Finally, the playfully exhausted Mommy Giant says, "OK! OK! I'm going to fix you! I'm going to get out of bed and cook your favorite chocolate chip pancakes for breakfast!" Finding her slippers and robe, she mutters in the children's hearing range, "That should make the little humans really sorry for waking me up!" as she walks to the kitchen.

Permitting your child to suddenly awaken you and expect a playful romping game to start off every day would be out of the question. However, *one* morning occasionally will do a world of good in building a healthy relationship with your child.

Do you do anything fun and out of the ordinary with your youngster when it is time to get up? Setting boundaries of appropriate times and occasions for a little romp in the morning is very important. Agree to rascally fun only if the bedroom door is wide open for the early bird riser to enter. You could set the alarm in an older child's room as the time to come and playfully get you up.

The Sleepy Sailor
Companionship Game of Adventure

Returning to the family, what else is happening? All the household is stirring, except for the five-year-old son. He is the night owl of the family who can literally hoot the evening hours away in playful activity. Getting him to go to sleep is difficult; getting him to wake up is a bigger challenge. After checking the other children, Daddy decides to be creative in waking his sleepy morning riser.

The father tiptoes into his son's bedroom and quietly snuggles under the blanket. "Time to get up, Matey!" he whispers. "Ship's leaving port. No landlubbers on board."

The child gruffs, rolls over, and tries to ignore the dad's playful comment. The father jiggles the ship bed by bouncing up and down and snuggles closer to his son like crowded shipmates might on a seagoing vessel.

"I feel a wind picking up!" Taking a handful of cloth, the dad billows up the sail sheet and begins it down over both heads. "Ahh! A nice dark cabin in case there's a storm." And he jiggles the bed noticeably as if a storm is coming.

"Hope we don't hit rough water!" pretends the father with concern. "If this old tug capsizes, we'll land in the ocean!" He bounces the bed, billows out the sheet several times, and playfully wrestles his waking son off the bed and onto the carpet as if a pretend storm has hit. Standing up, the father acts out swimming strokes toward the bathroom or kitchen.

"Come on, Matey! We'll make it to land! Keep swimming!" he calls over his shoulder to his young shipmate. If the son is slow getting up, a playful in-character action is for the dad to make believe a rescue of his floundering companion from the stormy wave carpet. Scooping up his child, he carries him out the door, all the time tickling him into a laughing, wiggling heap.

The Tootsie Toe
Opposite Game of Endearment

For this family, it's a busy morning! After mixing up the chocolate chip pancakes, Mom hears her fourteen-month-old daughter stirring in the crib. Preparing a bottle of milk, she goes to the child and greets one cute little girl with one smelly little diaper.

The little fourteen-month-old needs a diaper change. She securely holds her bottle, and her feet touch the bottle as Mom snugly positions a fresh diaper.

The mother gently pulls at the bottle as if to uncork her daughter's mouth, "Oh, please give me that yummy baby bottle!" Pretending to pull harder, the mother gives a little tickle to her daughter's tummy, making her laugh a sweet smile as she sucks harder and holds the bottle quite firmly in her baby grasp.

"Oh, you little rascal! Well, if I can't have your bottle, I'll nibble on your cute, sweet toes!" the mother declares. Scooping up her freshly changed infant, she gently nibbles the child's toes as if enjoying a delicious dessert.

"Ohhh! Your tootsie toes are so yummy, but they're still there! I want to gobble them up. Give me your cute toes right now!" pleads the young mother as she tries again and again to lovingly nibble up her child's ten delicious toes.

Laughing with delight at the attention and the tickle feeling, the child continues sucking the bottle and purposefully wiggles her feet close to the mother's face, trying to tempt her into another nibbling contest. The infant is playfully winning over the adult, and the power struggle between parent and child is creatively being defused a bit more in real life.

Little Kitchen Helper
Companionship Game of Adventure

Returning to the kitchen, the mother deposits her daughter in the high chair and places a handful of plain round dry cereal on the tray to keep her content.

The six-year-old is especially hungry this morning, which is probably why she woke up so early. Giving her a fun job to do might help occupy her until the breakfast is ready.

"Let's pretend our kitchen table is a big circus at the fair," suggests the mother. "The plates and glasses will be people lined up to see the show," she says out loud as she arranges the place settings around the table. "You put a fork on one side of each people plate and I'll put a napkin on the other." The mother helps the six-year-old place a fork to the left as she places a napkin to the right. "Hurray! Now everything is ready! I'll put the food on the table. Go call everyone to breakfast so the circus can begin," playfully instructs the mother as she serves up the food.

The French Restaurant
Variation of the Little Kitchen Helper

The mother and child could pretend an impersonation that would creatively use the child's energy and industry.

With animation, the mother pushes up her robe sleeves and waves her hand with a flurry of excitement like a professional French chef in an exclusive dining establishment.

"Ahh, Mademoiselle, please come quick! These expensive china dishes need to be placed upon the table," she says with an accent and hands the child a stack of paper plates, cups, and some of the eating utensils.

The family will soon be called to the table. The child is helping to set out the food, plates, and eating utensils.

"Mademoiselle, are the customers' places ready? You know we always want happy customers coming to our restaurant!" reminds the mother with mock seriousness in her voice.

"Here, do set these carefully on the table," she instructs with flair. Handing the child the forks to be placed by the plates, she says, "Left side. Always they go on the left side by the napkin.

"Lovely job, Mademoiselle. A perfectly lovely job! I will speak to Monsieur about the tip today," promises the mother as she invites the daughter to join the family at the table.

An excellent work ethic is playfully being taught to a young child. Doing a simple job carefully, accurately, and well receives praise and sometimes also a reward. The mother may pretend a secretive whisper to Daddy about the daughter's willingness, effort, and actual performance—anything positive that can be genuinely praised.

The father may choose to single out his daughter with a sincere compliment and even place a quarter tip in her eager little palm as a tangible thank-you for being a wonderful little helper to her mommy.

The Father's Version of Little Kitchen Helper

The father becomes the wagon train's crusty older cook stirring up vittles for the cowhands on Saturday morning. Talking with a Texas drawl, he enlists their help in getting out paper plates, cups, and napkins. He calls them the old tin plates and mugs on the cattle drive.

Chairs are pushed up to the counter, and the children are allowed to stir eggs cracked in a bowl. These are the wild chicken eggs found inside the cactus refrigerator at the last stop by Dry Gulch.

Talking about roping and branding ornery weather-beaten steers, the father cooks the vittles over the campfire. When all is ready, his cowhands sit cross-legged on the rugged kitchen tile and eat their egg-and-beef jerky bacon breakfast while he talks about a pretend or real trip out west.

For cleanup time, the father pushes chairs up to the counter, and they wash the cooking utensils in the sudsy river sink.

The creative father and his children have wonderfully pretended and experienced a great day on the Texas range. They had fun in working together to get a job done. Feeding the kids their breakfast while Mom sleeps late on Saturday morning is creatively etched on the hearts and memories of the youngsters.

Plate Face Delight
Opposite Game of Adventure

Back at the kitchen table, the family gathers for the chocolate chip pancake breakfast. The mother cooked the pancakes extra small, about the size of a quarter. She decided to make a face with the pancakes and bacon. Three little pancakes make the eyes and nose of the face, and the bacon shapes the mouth.

The mother remembered that making a clown's face on the children's plates delighted them. Her three-year-old daughter, who is a picky eater, ate breakfast so well that day!

The food is arranged on the plates in the shape of a smiling clown face. The cinnamon toast is cut in triangles, making the two eyes; the small pile of eggs makes the clown's big nose; the bacon makes his happy smile.

"Good morning, Mr. Clown! I'm so glad your smiling face brightens up our day!" cheerfully greets the mother. "Eat your breakfast, children."

As the three-year-old picks up her piece of cinnamon toast, the mother pretends a laughing voice as if the clown face plate were actually speaking: "Good morning, little lady. I'm glad to meet you."

The child giggles with delight at the idea of a talking plate. She bites again.

The three-year-old knows Mommy is making the plate's voice. She laughs at the idea and fun of a talking plate.

Little Pooski Pooh Pie
Companionship Game of Endearment

The breakfast is over. Before the dirty dishes are cleaned off the kitchen table, the newborn baby cries from her cradle to be picked up and fed. "Ahhh, the newborn!" the young mother sighs with love and a little weariness as she walks to the baby's bed.

Cuddling her little bundle, the mother sits in her rocking chair to rest and nurse her baby. Daddy is home and watches the other children; there is no hurry.

"Good morning to you, you little rascal. Didn't you just eat a few hours ago?" the mother gently chides. "Well, I suppose my Little Pooski Pooh Pie gets hungry, too," croons the mother as she pats her baby's chubby legs, keeping time with rocking.

You're Pooski Pooh Pie short and stout.
Here is your tummy. Oh, it pokes out!
When you get all steamed up, yes, you shout!
You're my Pooski Pooh Pie short and stout.

The mother quietly sings the nonsensical ditty to the tune of "I'm a Little Teapot." Accentuating each stanza by a gentle pat, the mother feels the baby nestle closer to her.

The Bandit Clothes
Companionship Game of Adventure

The three-year-old and five-year-old have been fed. During the week the father leaves for work and takes the oldest to kindergarten. The mother begins her busy day.

"OK, Deputies! We've got to bring them in!" alerts the mother as she pretends to be the brave sheriff of Neatness Nook, a very respectable place where lots of good folks live.

"I suspect they're hiding in your drawers and closet! Don't worry! We'll get them!" she instructs the children to follow her to their bedroom.

The children look fascinated at their mother. "What is she talking about? What is she doing?" they wonder as she opens a dresser drawer, sneaking a peek inside. Suddenly, she grabs a faded pair of blue socks. Shaking them in her hand, she acts as if they are alive, squirming and struggling to get away.

"Yes! I got them! I caught the Blue Bandit socks! They're a tricky pair, always disappearing in the washing machine! I got them both this time," she declares triumphantly.

"Now that we've captured these bandit socks, we've got to keep up with them. Hey! Let's put them on your feet, Deputy! That'll keep them safe!" she suggests.

Sitting down on the floor, she puts her five-year-old in her lap and tells him what a brave boy he is for arresting the old blue socks: "Why, if they're stuck inside your shoes, they'll never get loose all day!

"Shoes? Where are the bandit tennis shoes hiding?" she asks. "They're in the closet or perhaps under the bed!" She crawls on all fours to the closet as if to sneak up and spy on them.

"Quick, go and find them before they try to get away," the mother insists. All of Neatness Nook is depending on them, the brave sheriff and deputies, to capture the bandit clothes and get them on their bodies before sundown.

"Clothes! Where are all your clothes hiding?" she exclaims.

Tiger Towels and Panda Pants
Companionship Game of Adventure

The three-year-old and five-year-old are dressed and playing with their building blocks in the family room. The babies are napping. The mother does some housework until her five-year-old, who misses his big sister at kindergarten, wanders into the laundry room and says, "There's nothing for me to do!"

"Help me tame the tiger towels and save the panda pants. And then you can help me bake cookies for lunch," coaxes the mother as she continues folding.

"What tigers and pandas?" asks her son.

"Why, the ferocious tiger dish and bathroom towels lurking behind the clean clothes!" says the mother with a frightened voice.

"The poor panda pants are very afraid of being eaten up!" sadly remarks the mother and drops her hands as if discouraged about the situation.

"The tiger towels don't like being stuck in kitchen drawers and in the bathroom away from the sweet children who live here. They want to be close to you, like the panda pants. Think of all the fun your play clothes have when they are on you and you are playing outside!" says the mother with mock seriousness in her voice and a merry twinkle in her eye.

"Dear me, I have quite a lot of trouble with them! Will you help me?" she sincerely asks her youngster. "If we put them away, we can bake some yummy cookies together!"

Before the child has a chance to answer, the playful mother catches a mischievous yellow washcloth and make believes it is alive and growling as she firmly folds its four corners.

Baking Buddy Brigade
Companionship Game of Adventure

The young son did a wonderful job folding the clothes. The mother decides he will mainly oversee the cookies being mixed and baked. It's ten o'clock, and the children are clamoring for a snack.

"Captain, the troops are hungry! Shall we get everybody fed?" asks the mother as she respectfully salutes her son and marches to the kitchen with a stiff soldier's stride.

"Hup, two! Hup, two! Hup, two!" she playfully barks out like a tough sergeant to the children gleefully following.

"Hurry it up, everybody!" the mother insists as if talking to a troop of privates.

The mother gathers up all cookie ingredients that her five-year-old can successfully handle and lines them in a straight line like soldiers standing at attention. She sets the more difficult items inconspicuously to the side.

"All present, Sir!" she states. "Shall we begin the maneuvers, Sir?"

Allowing her son to measure, pour, and stir the ingredients in the mixing bowl adds to his feeling of being in charge of the difficult, even dangerous, cooking maneuver. (Sometimes a very disorderly fresh egg will roll off the counter and break to pieces!)

The little captain allows the little privates a taste of the batter and is encouraged to share some of the mixing maneuvers with them. Letting her son and daughter push the batter off the spoon and onto the cookie sheet makes them feel together as buddies in baking.

"Sir, cookies are prepared for the oven. Shall I dismiss the troops until they're ready for eating?" requests the mother.

Tops and Bottoms and Things
Companionship Game of Adventure

After a light snack, the three-year-old and five-year-old bound off to play, and the fourteen-month-old is allowed to explore the kitchen while the mother cleans up.

One kitchen cabinet is set aside for the children's grown-up cooking things. Assorted tops and bottoms from old plastic containers are stored here along with unbreakable discarded kitchen items—perhaps a dented little skillet, mismatched measuring cups, wooden spoons, anything a toddler can grab, bang, stack, and harmlessly engage in play.

"Sweetheart, it's time you cooked something," the mother suggests. "I'll get you started." She begins stacking the plastic containers pyramid style or one inside the other.

"Ohh! Look how high they are!" or "Where did they all go?" she may wonder out loud to her child, prodding her toddler to copy the feat.

"Do you need some food to cook?" observes the mother. "I'll put goodies [raisins, pretzels, crackers] inside the containers. You cook them into a delicious meal."

The mother seals a small amount of the goodies inside the plastic containers and then shakes the containers to draw the child's interest. Stacking them, the mother leaves the child to open them and prepare, cook, and eat the pretend meal.

Read Me a Story
Opposite Game of Endearment

The children are getting a little tired from the busy morning. The mother decides they all need rest.

The young mother and her children lie down in the same bed or vicinity.

"Mommy [or Daddy], please read me five stories. Please! I'll be very quiet!" playfully begs the young mother to one of her resting children.

Before lying down, she secured a supply of familiar storybooks from the bookshelf. The child who is going to be the parent is allowed to pick the books she or he wants and is encouraged to read or pretend to read any of the picture stories.

"Let me see the pictures, please," sweetly requests the young mother.

The child holds up the book for all to see. The mother eagerly asks, "What's that and that?" She points at the skinny monkey, the big banana tree, and the pile of bananas pictured on the storybook page.

The mother does this in a rascally manner, perhaps pitching her voice high like a child's or behaving with childlike animation and exuberance. The mother's motion will be a teasing enticement for the child to have to remind the mother that this is to be a restful time.

"It's a monkey and some fruit! Now you have to be quiet and hold still if you want me to read this story to you. Be a good girl!" patiently commands the child to her mother.

With the child's first reminder, the mother settles down and obediently folds her hands in her lap and listens quietly, relishing the moments of peaceful rest and inactivity the little mommy requires.

Lunch Under the Table
Opposite Game Blended with Companionship Game

Getting up from rest time, the family is ready for lunch. Today it is sunny outside, perfect for a picnic in the backyard. The two older children drag the old comforter to the picnic table. The mother makes a tray of peanut butter-and-jelly sandwiches, cut carrots, and a pitcher of juice and goes outside.

The children watch as their mother fluffs the comforter over the picnic table and then crawls under the covered table fort.

(That is the first opposite feature: reversing the normal way of eating at the table.)

"Quick! Get inside now! They might see us!" she says with mock concern as she lifts up an edge of the comforter and beckons for the children to follow.

"Who might?" ask her inquisitive three, darting under the comforter.

"Why, the birds or squirrels might come along and want our food! We've got to eat it before they find us! There's no telling how hungry they might be!" explains the mother as she hands the very important food items to her children. The mother might steal a peek outside the comforter to make sure that no animal is sneaking up. She could whisper a hungry "peep" for emphasis or say, "Shoo to you!" as if waving away a make-believe animal.

"You know, forts always protect you from something! Our fort protects us from all those hungry little critters outside who want our food," continues the mother as she weaves a story about real or invisible and make-believe animals who might want to gobble up the children's lunch before they do. (These are the second and third opposite features: timid animals do not stalk, and children do not generally guard their food.)

The Whying
Opposite Game of Adventure

The children have finished eating lunch. The baby needs to be fed. The mother decides to occupy her older youngsters while nursing her little daughter. She encourages her children to be inquisitive problem solvers.

Most two-, three-, four-, and five-year-old children constantly ask questions during the early formative years. Reverse this pattern. Mentally engage a youngster with so many interesting *why* questions that he begins to plead, "Please stop asking me so many questions for a while! I need to rest!"

The young mother spreads the comforter under a shady tree in the backyard. Resting against the tree, she comfortably settles the baby and asks her children a simple question.

"Why do cats meow?" the mother wonders.

"Well, Mommy, that's just the way they talk," offers one child.

"Oh! I'm glad to know that!" enthusiastically responds the mother. "Why do they want to talk?" she continues to wonder.

"Maybe they talk when they're hungry," suggests another.

Satisfied with the reasoning, the mother goes on to another question: "But why do you think they climb trees?"

"They like to, like us!" is a giggly response.

Looking up at the trees, the mother notices one high branch brushing against a large electric utility wire and points it out with a question: "Why are electric wires high up in the air on those big poles?"

Gazing at the wires high overhead, the children think for a moment. One child finally says, "I don't know."

"Just guess!" coaxes his mother.

"So people won't trip over the wires" is the child's solution.

"That's a good answer! You know, if a person touched just one of those big cables with one tiny finger, it would shock him very badly! ZZZing and he might be dead!" emphasizes the mother by making a sizzling sound as she speaks.

"Nooo," respond the children with wide-eyed awe.

"Yes! Never touch electric wires outside on poles," she instructs.

"But why are those wires there?" continues the mother.

"For birds to sit on?" offers one youngster.

"Good thinking! Yes, birds sit on them and squirrels, too. The wires bring electricity to our home so we can turn on our lights," explains the mother. Then with a rascally gleam, she innocently asks, "Why can little animals touch the wires and not get hurt?"

The whying game continues until child or parent tires of asking questions. Generally, the child will weary first because his thinking skills have been used and exercised more fully than usual.

The game may stop because neither knows the answer, which is a great opportunity to lead a child to solve a problem by further investigation. Look up the answer in a book, or ask another person. If that person is the other parent, the child has been creatively directed to have continued and meaningful parental contact. If a young child's intellect is truly engaged in the whying game, she will probably want to discover the answer out of sheer curiosity.

This is an excellent game to play on a family trip when children are confined to a small space and boredom sets in. Ask,

- "Why does the painted line in the middle of the road shine at night?"
- "Why are the road lines sometimes broken and sometimes solid?"
- "Why does the car ahead blink its red taillights when it slows?"
- "Why do roads have land or walls between cars going different ways?"
- "Why are there signs with big numbers on them?"
- "Why are city buildings made of bricks and concrete?"
- "Why are weather vanes on barn roofs?"
- "Why are deserts brown and not green?"
- "Why is salt put on the icy highway?"

"Why? Why? Why?" continues to ask the parent as one interesting question is answered by the child after another until even her inquisitive tendency is satisfied, and she finally says, "Please don't ask me any more questions!"

The first time a child expresses the desire to stop answering questions, you should stop. Otherwise, the good bonding effect developing between you and your child in this opposite game may be spoiled.

Attempting to playfully engage a child in creative problem solving is an excellent way to strengthen his thinking skills and tire him out at the same time. Generally, a child wants to play more quietly after having thoroughly exercised the mind in an interesting and challenging way. Creating an intriguing mental game is a great way to promote more physical peace and quiet in a child's life and yours as well.

Little Plane Pilot
Companionship Game of Endearment

Returning to the family in the backyard, it is getting hot, and the children want to go inside. The picnic lunch is gathered up, and all march like soldiers into the house. "Hup, two! Hup, two!" they chant as they throw away trash and march to the bathroom to wash their hands.

The baby goes to bed. The other children entertain themselves in the family room. After a short time, an argument breaks out between the children. The toddler topples the block house the other two worked hard to build. "Mommy! Mommy! Get the baby! She's messing up everything!" cry both older children.

The mother retrieves the fourteen-month-old who is now screaming with disappointment at being lifted away from the colorful blocks and her little playmates. To divert her attention, the mother holds the child securely overhead and flies her through the air as if she is a soaring plane.

"Zzzooommm! Away we go!" says the mother as she whirls her child in the motion of a soaring plane.

"Let's fly high and fast!" she exclaims, lifting her little daughter first high overhead and then zooming her down low through the air.

"Rrrooommm! We're off!" she calls, walking out of the family room.

Turning in circles several times and bouncing the child up and down, the mother finally coasts her to a stop and then gives a big hug.

"We made it to the kitchen, and you get a bottle!" the mother promises as she holds her toddler while pouring a bottle full of cold milk from the refrigerator.

There are countless variations of creatively distracting a very young child from a disruptive situation. You could privately whisper something like this in a child's ear: "Come on with me, Sweetheart. We're going to do something really fun! Just you and me!" You offer a pleasant alternative for you and your child to enjoy together.

Such temporary and interesting distractions defuse sibling conflicts and build the one-on-one emotional bonding so vital between parent and child.

Make-Believe Games
for the Afternoon and Evening

Early afternoon means time for a rest. The younger children are easier to get to bed; the older ones are beginning to outgrow their second rest time in one day. Getting her energetic youngsters in the vicinity of the bedroom, the mother calls them to join in a game she wants to play. Entering the room, they see her lightly bouncing on the side of the bed.

The Train Ride
Companionship Game of Adventure

"I'm going on a train ride!" she excitedly announces. Then she extends an invitation: "Want to go with me?" Patting the mattress beside her in a welcoming gesture, she continues gently bouncing up and down and holds her arms out in front of her as if holding the throttle of the train. With deep concentration, she squeezes her outstretched hands tightly and intently gazes ahead with the serious business of conducting a passenger express train down the railroad tracks.

"Yeah!" chorus the children as they scamper up on the bed.

"My, I love train rides. See those trees and houses and fields fly by. Oh, look over there at those cute little calves! Do you see them? What color are they?" The mother looks and points out make-believe things of interest while continuing to bounce up and down.

"Oh, I see them! They're white with black spots and they're brown," respond the children to the mother's coaxing.

"Well, I hope no cow gets on the train track. Hey! Want to blow the whistle? Here, pull this!" The mother pulls down on an invisible lever above her head and says, "Choo, choo, choo!"

"Choo, choo, choo!" mimic the children as they pull the invisible lever.

"Would you like to be the engineer? First one and then the other. I'll pull the whistle some more. Be very careful going around the curves." The mother moves both outstretched arms from in front of her body to in front of one child's body as if she is giving him the controls. She pulls down on the invisible whistle lever, says, "Choo, choo, choo!" and bounces higher, leaning her body to the side as if the train is on a turn.

"I'm the engineer!" laughs the child excitedly as he follows his mother and holds his arms out in front, bounces on the bed, and leans to the side, pretending to be taking a curve, too.

"Look out! There's a cow on the track up ahead! Slow the train down before we hit her!" alerts the mother with mock concern and excitement. She slows her bouncing on the bed until she is sitting still. "Shoo cow! Off the track!" commands the mother, pretending to wave away the cow.

"Shoo cow! Shoo! Shoo!" say the children as they imitate their mother and pretend to wave the cow off the track.

"My, I'm so glad that cow wasn't hurt!" says the mother in relief. She dabs her forehead as if wiping away nervous sweat. "Well, let's get going again," she says brightly and begins bouncing up and down on the bed, her eyes gazing ahead. "Know where we're going?" she questions.

"No. Where are we going?" they respond.

"Oh, Kalamazoo or Timbuktu maybe," she answers cheerfully and uses her imagination to describe these exotic places while continuing to point out scenic landscape along the way. Finally, she says, "We'll be there soon. We'll have cookies and milk after getting off the train.

"Here's the train station. Such a nice train ride," she comments, gives one last "choo, choo, choo," slows down bouncing on the bed until she is sitting still, then drops her hands in her lap and looks around.

"Well, we're here! Let's get off the train and find some cookies and milk. Watch your step," the mother instructs and takes the children by the hand and carefully gets up from the bed.

The make-believe train ride is a companionship game that uses a high degree of imagery and imagination. Keeping simple body movements while weaving a good story line allows even a young child to engage in the game. Two children were successfully included in the playtime because there was individual action for each to share and do.

The train ride is an advanced saga of adventure for a young child. Initially, you may have to coach your child as to appropriate playful responses in pretending to conduct a train since the experience being imitated may not be familiar. Read illustrated books about trains to teach in-character action.

The Best Boxes Ever
Companionship Game

Rest time is over, and the children are up. The afternoon is spent in working, playing, and developing friendships. The children love to pretend with cardboard boxes.

Several clean cardboard boxes are secured from the grocery store. They become covered wagons, tree-barked Indian canoes, and wooden pirate vessels of yesterday; cars, planes, trains, and boats of today; or manned spaceships to Mars, capsules descending to the earth's center, and ocean bottom research labs of tomorrow.

Colorful wheels, sails, or figures may be drawn on the sides, control panels designed on the flaps, or holes punched through and string tied to connect several boxes. The child may decorate her own special box, or the adult and the child may create something together. However, once construction is finished and the child sits inside her make-believe transportation, the magic begins.

"Vroom! You're off! Oh, do be careful, Sweetheart!" The mother waves good-bye to her fearless explorer as he and his box assume the character of another time and place. She stays in character for the duration of the child's creative playtime.

Should the child imagine himself a fearless jungle explorer going down the Amazon on a wooden raft, he is referred to as the famous Professor Whatsit (or any nonsensical but catchy name). He or the adult jostles, shakes, and swirls the box boat as if it is a real river-worthy raft going down the Amazon.

In-character sights, sounds, and happenings are imagined and brought to life by both child and adult. The mother may walk through the living room with an arm full of clean folded clothes and pretend a frightened scream, duck her head, and cry out, "Professor Whatsit, save me! That big water snake is swimming toward us!" After frantically pointing out the snake, she runs from the room in mock fright.

Any imagined events should not really frighten or alarm a child. You should attempt to engineer fun happenings that fan the child's imagination. Whistling like a chattering jungle parrot and swinging one's arms like a gorilla passing by are good in-character touches for a jungle fantasy.

You should attempt to trigger rather than take over the child's creative expression. You could quietly and inconspicuously drop colorful building blocks around the child's box raft and then exclaim, "Look at all those pretty fish swimming in the water! I wonder if we could catch them for dinner?"

Household Hideout
Companionship Game of Adventure

Returning to the household, the three oldest children are looking for something interesting and different to do. The mother decides to play with them in a make-believe getaway time.

"Quick! Come with me!" whispers the mother and beckons them to follow her into the bedroom closet. "It's time for our special meeting," she explains with hushed secrecy in her voice.

"What meeting?" excitedly ask the children. "What are we doing in the closet?" they wonder out loud.

"The special meeting of Kids in the Closet is officially called to order. Is everyone here?" asks the mother and then takes roll call. "We have a very important matter to decide. Shall we read a story first by flashlight and then eat our cheese and crackers? Or shall we eat first and then read? You three decide." The mother has brought along a flashlight, storybook, and cheese and crackers in a bag.

A variation of the household hideout involves selecting a secret place, such as under the dining room table or behind the sofa. Pretend to be escaping humans from the giants who have already captured the other children and now are looking for you both. Have on hand colorful candy or fruit bits as treasure you've found in the underground cave where you, as lost explorers, have mysteriously fallen. How will you get out? What will you do? Invent as many vivid exploits as possible to spellbind your youngster in a special singled-out time of creative play.

Mr. Russel-Snussel Bear
Opposite Game of Adventure

The father is home now, and it's near suppertime. While the mother finishes meal preparations, the father distracts the children.

Mr. Russel-Snussel Bear is a big roly-poly bear who loves to catch little giggly children and playfully toss them on his couch cave. There they must stay until a little brother or sister touches and releases them to scamper back to the safety of some other piece of furniture that's home base. Mr. Russel-Snussel Bear growls fiercely whenever a child comes near him; he swirls and sways on all fours with make-believe menace; he swats with a big gentle paw, trying to catch a child's retreating body.

Sometimes, all the children attack him at once and smother his big frame with hugs, holds, and squeezes. Does he ever roar with make-believe anger and frustration! What trembling tingles of excitement they feel at capturing the giant bear! How will they ever get back to the safety of home base now that he's cornered?

Perhaps sly old Mr. Russel-Snussel is lying very, very still under their heaped little bodies because he's going to bounce up suddenly and grab one particular child in a great big bear hug while the others successfully get away! Who really knows what he'll do next? The children dance around him, wondering with delight.

Rug Wrestlers
Opposite Game of Adventure

After supper, the five-year-old wants to feel big and to be in charge of something, like his oldest sister gets to do. The father senses his son's frustration and decides to help him feel like a champ at something.

The father measures off a section of carpet and uses throw pillows to mark the four corners of the wrestling ring. Or an area rug in the family room may be just the right size for the world championship wrestling match about to begin.

The father flexes his arms while kneeling down at the child's eye level and gives a playful challenge to his little son: "So you're famous Slick Slammer who's defeated every last wrestler in the East and now you're trying to move into my territory?

"Why, I bet if we wrestled right now, you'd have a pretty hard time beating me!" the father boasts in a playful attempt to get his son to accept the man-to-man challenge. The father might say, "Here's my hand. Just see if you can pin me!" Then lying on his stomach, the father offers a preliminary hand wrestling contest, just to show how strong he is.

With mock struggle and effort the boastful adult is humiliated and defeated within seconds by the little boy. Feigning shock and embarrassment, the father puffs out his chest and exclaims, "Well, arm wrestling doesn't count! You've got a pin all of me on that carpet if you're really the winner!"

The son's masculinity is fanned a bit by the win, and he accepts his father's continued challenge.

As father and son wrestle, the father holds his child securely with one arm and rolls over on him while supporting his entire weight with the other arm. As his child struggles and pushes, the father flings himself over as if being toppled by the child.

The father pretends to be the television broadcaster commenting on the match: "And Slick Slammer just landed a sudden waist flip to his opponent, Big Body, who seems stunned by the quick maneuver!"

As the wrestling match continues, the father pretends signs of weakening and growing weary. He staggers around the ring as if overwhelmed by his powerful opponent. Finally, with a surge of energy, the father makes a bold attempt to pin his son and allows himself to be overcome and toppled backward in defeat.

The little son cheers himself with a victory dance, which is heightened by the father's mock disappointment, humiliation, and defeat. "I'm the winner!" he beams as he feels the thrill, excitement, and fun of playfully pinning his daddy in a fantasy contest.

Daddy Donkey
Opposite Game of Adventure

The girls want to join their father, and they clamor for his attention. Since he is being a little rambunctious anyway, the father decides to play one more active game that singles out each child, and then their romping playtime is over for the evening.

The father gets on all fours and assumes the character of the Daddy Donkey the children love. Tonight, he pretends to be a very lively animal who playfully rears up, whirls in circles, and tries to wiggle the first laughing youngster off his back. With the next child, the father becomes the sly old critter who one minute lies down as if sound asleep and the next tries to playfully buck off his young rider. With the third child, he becomes stubborn and won't budge unless he is sweetly patted on the nose, fed a pretend carrot, and told he's a good old boy! And then he gives that child a fast, smooth ride around the dining room table.

The father creates as many in-character donkey qualities and personalities as he can. He attempts to playfully spellbind his young brood by giving each child individual attention in a group activity. As every child gets a turn, each experiences fun and success in handling their creative make-believe Daddy Donkey.

Bedtime is quickly arriving for the younger children. The babies are down. As the two middle children are changing into their pajamas, the mother pulls down the sheets and shapes the pillows into a roundish-looking nest in the middle of each bed. "What are you doing, Mommy?" both ask. "Quick, brush your teeth, and I'll tell you," promises the mother. Then she plays the baby bird companionship game (see chapter 9).

Bedtime arrives for the oldest child, and Mother comes to tuck her in. Before reading the children's illustrated Bible story and saying prayers, the mother creatively weaves a playful activity (the belly button eraser opposite game from chapter 11) with which to close down the busy day.

Creative Make-Believe and Loving Relationships

The day is over. The family members have spent a good portion of it being relational and involved with each other. Little and big ones have been won over to a more loving relationship through creatively playing together. Quality time was spent in weaving love and memories into each other's lives, and precious human hearts were captured as best friends. Power struggles between child and adult were more defused as Mother and Father purposefully engineered creative fun and successes for their youngsters to experience.

You can use every imaginative activity described in this chapter with your family. The ideas and incentives of creative play can be altered to fit specific childhood needs. For any family, however, creative play needs to be a balanced and reasonable form of communication. Engaging in too much could become mentally and physically exhausting to you, and engaging in too little could dispirit and distance your child. Somedays only one make-believe game may be played; some days several; some days none. You need to willingly pace healthy interaction and use creative play to advance the relationship rather than wear out the participants.

New friends, experiences, and surroundings quickly broaden your elementary-age child's world. Elementary age is the time for processing and maturing. Creative play greatly helps both you and your child to strengthen relational bonding during this growing-up phase.

Creative Make-Believe for an Elementary-Age Child

With an elementary-age child, you must master how to translate your past playful tendency into present creative play. Past creativity must meaningfully affect the older child's present life and circumstances. You need to update creative playfulness with games that match the maturation level of your older child.

An elementary-age child, though notably formed and influenced by the age of five, continues to be impressionable, and you still have a great opportunity to affect your child's personality. You have excellent prospects of connecting with your child's heart in a loving relationship.

Know Your Elementary-Age Child

For the purposes of this chapter, we'll consider an elementary-age child to be six to ten years of age. You must recognize this age span and work creatively with it rather than against it, especially when engaging in playful creativity with your child. Chronological age and maturation age may be vastly different in your child. That is one reason why an older child may behave with such childish qualities.

Creative play is based primarily on a child's emotional maturation and secondarily on chronological age. This is especially true with an elementary-age child. Although the actual age of the child is important, it is not the foremost factor to be considered in playing creatively.

Interwoven with chronological age and emotional maturation are the child's God-given imagination and innate creative ability. At times, a child's creative talent may have little or nothing to do with actual age or emotional maturation. Humans are creative beings because God's creativity is breathed within them. Expressing God-given creativity does not necessarily depend on the skills and abilities acquired while maturing.

Communication that reaches the heart necessitates your knowing your elementary-age child. What maturation level is the child? Is it the same as her chronological age? Why? What innate talents does she possess and express?

Answering these questions will help you construct and pace playful activities that coincide with your child's emotional level. The imaginative and creative play taps and flourishes the child's true emotional base. Your child will naturally begin to leave behind make-believe games that emotionally are too young for him to enjoy. The child should not be expected at age ten to enthusiastically embrace games he enjoyed at age six.

Connecting with your child's heart occurs more easily when you hit the mark rather than overshoot or undershoot being playfully engaged with your elementary-age child.

Hit the Mark by Targeting the Fun, Friendship, and Fantasy Factors

To spellbind an elementary-age child through creative play, keep in mind the fun, friendship, and fantasy factors. Whatever make-believe games you introduce need to hit the mark on all three counts. Your child will be quick to let you know if the make-believe game is off target; his interest level, body language, and comments will almost instantly tell you if you missed the mark. If you overshoot his emotional level and introduce a game too mature or complicated for him to enjoy, he will probably express confusion, disinterest, frustration, or boredom. If you undershoot his emotional level and introduce a game too immature for him to play, he will more than likely comment, "Oh, that's babyish! I don't want to play that anymore!" His body language will definitely indicate his embarrassment, irritation, or even disgust at being treated like a baby.

You may need to teach a hesitant or unsure child how to play creatively or be healthily stretched beyond her too narrow comfort zone. You need great sensitivity in determining what is causing your child to be resistant to creative play. Is it due to your misjudging your child's emotional level or to your child's having a selfish attitude?

Besides considering the child's emotional level, you need to be aware of the other factors affecting her. Do these influences affect her positively or negatively? Do they help or hinder her in healthy emotional bonding with you? Attempt to work creatively with the positive external influences and against the negative ones. To hit this target, you need to know your child's world.

Know Your Elementary-Age Child's World

Elementary age indicates a growing and formative period; ideas and skills first encountered in the younger years are being tested and perfected. The little novice individual is developing into a more seasoned person with whom to reckon. The child's world and relationships extend beyond parents, immediate family, and special caregivers to the neighborhood, peers, school, and the larger world.

Because your child's world has broadened, you no longer remain the exclusive and necessarily most significant person in the child's life. You have powerful competition drawing on the heart and affection of your child. These influences can be healthy and positive or destructive and negative. A peer can become a dear friend who challenges and encourages the child through every stage of life. A gifted teacher may instill such a love of learning that the child is early drawn to a lifelong profession. The child's positive heart attachments are very beneficial, and you should welcome and encourage them. Likewise, external negative influences can damage your child's ability to make a good heart attachment to you.

Timing wholesome creative play with your elementary-age child will work wonders in keeping or reestablishing a healthy relationship. To help you in this endeavor, come and spend a summer with the Boswells' elementary-age children. Experience creative play updated and matched with the general emotional levels of elementary-age children.

All creative make-believe games introduced in this chapter as summertime adventures were played throughout the year. Summer for many families means more free time, a slower schedule in many ways, and a quieter portion of the year in some respects. But whenever you have calmer moments—fall, spring, or winter; after school, before bedtime, or on Saturdays— you need to seize the priceless moments and create a memory in your relationship with your child.

Spend a Summer Together

It's summertime and all the children are at home, the elementary-age ones looking forward to the seemingly endless three months of fun and freedom. The oldest is ten; the latest addition is thirteen months. The children playfully scamper inside and outside the house, plotting as many intriguing exploits as their creative little minds can invent.

Mud Pies
Companionship Game of Adventure

"Blub, blub, blub," sputters the baby brother as he tries to swim like a porpoise in the shallow wading pool. The oldest daughter continues manning the garden hose as her eight-year-old sister takes a turn at swimming across the ocean and splashes out the other side.

"Hey! Let's do something different now!" suggests the seven-year-old as she wiggles her toes in the muddy dirt beside the wading pool. Patting the oozy earth, she scoops up two big handfuls and starts to fling the mud at her near twin six-year-old sister who is sitting contentedly in the cool water.

Just then their mother walks out the back door. "Don't throw it!" she firmly cautions. Emptying her young daughter's muddy hands, she washes them off with the garden hose and thinks up a creative alternative.

"Hey! Let's make mud pies instead of throwing the dirt, Sweetheart," suggests the mother, scooping up two big handfuls of mud and walking over to one of the cement squares forming the backyard walkway.

"Here's the oven. Now let's fix up these little mud pies really pretty and then cook them," the mother imagines out loud as she carefully patty-cakes the mud into roundish shapes on the concrete.

"Oh, dear, where are the dry sprinkle sand sugar and the green leaf nuts? We have to cook with them to make our mud pies tasty! Let's go find some," coaxes the mother as she and her daughter go hand in hand to look for the special ingredients for the child's delicious mud pies.

This creative and fun moment shared with a caring parent in the backyard deflected, defused, and completely avoided some possibly hostile influences. The child's natural curiosity and exploration in regard to the properties of wet earth weren't dampened. The rivalry of sisters only fourteen months apart wasn't fanned by excluding the seven-year-old from play for attempted rather than real misbehavior. The mother wasn't perceived as a truant officer rather than a best friend companion who was compassionate and kind and knew how to have fun. The adult and the child experienced the same childlike pleasures of handling mud and enjoyed a brief make-believe adventure with it and with each other.

Mixing Up the Mix
Opposite Game of Adventure

Summertime always finds the kids hungry! Their tummies seem bottomless; they love to sample and taste anything sweet Mother cooks. What a wonderful opportunity to allow them sweet success at winning over their parent!

"I'm going to make something sweet. Do you want to help me?" asks the mother as she places chairs along the kitchen counter so the children can add ingredients and stir the mixture in the bowl.

"I'm so glad you're here! I need your help to take care of our mixture. It's very temperamental. Stir carefully or it will become dough, and we'll have to bake it into cookies!" explains the mother with a worried look.

"If the soft butter blends with the sugar and the egg yolks break, our mixture will turn into dough. So be careful!" she explains as the children pick up on the playful twist and giggle about her cooking instructions.

"Oh dear! The mixture looks more like dough every minute with all your stirring! What happened to the vanilla and salt we just put in the bowl? And the chocolate chips are getting all covered up!" she frets as each child delights in taking a turn blending the mixture of ingredients into dough.

"If this keeps up, our pretty mixture will soon become cookie dough and we'll have to bake it! Oh dear, will that be all right with you?" she asks with pretend apology in her voice.

"Oh, thank you for keeping my cookie batter safe from all those little fingers trying to snitch it! You've all done such a great job! Here, Mommy wants each of you to have a little taste because you've all protected it so well!"

The mother rewards them for their vigilant guard, claiming each child an honored hero of the cookie batter.

"Well, Sweethearts, it's time to get down. I'll call you and you can help me again next time I bake cookies. I love you," comments the mother as she helps the last of her children down from the counter.

"I Love You! I Said It First! I Win!"
"Well, I Said It Second!"
Opposite Game of Endearment

Having the children around all day allows the mother to single out each child and create a playful contest that encourages the expression of love. (If your child is not accustomed to the "I love you!" game, read chapter 11 to familiarize yourself with it before trying to introduce the following added creative reverse.)

The children are accustomed to the "I love you!" game. To vary her defeat and construct a double win for them, the mother adds a new creative touch.

The mother allows her child to beat her at saying, "I love you!" This time, however, she maintains a winner's attitude and retorts, "Well, I love you, and I said it second! So there, I win!"

The child knows it is a false claim and win and will vigorously challenge the adult.

"Uh-uh! You said it second! You can't win!" contests the child, surprised that the parent would even try such a trick.

"Well, I'm going to tell your mother on you for winning! You'll be sorry!" sniffs the adult.

"You are my mother!" counters the child with delight at exposing the parent's absurd comment.

"Well, I'll fix you! I'm going to tell your older sister's mommy on you!" quickly counters the mother.

"You are her mother!" retorts the child, beginning to pick up on the direction of the contest.

"Well, I'm going to tell your older brother's mommy on you!" continues the mother.

"You are his mother!" laughs her fourth-in-line daughter, who fully expects the mother to go through the entire list of children in the family.

As the mother does just that, she ends with a pretended exasperated comment at being so thoroughly defeated in every way possible in the contest: "I can't possibly be all those mommies!"

"But you are all those mommies!" laughs her middle daughter with delight at having won over her mother in so many ways.

A more general double reverse of the "I love you! I said it second!" game would be the adult's use of the names by which she goes. For instance, once the child challenges the adult's fake win the second time, the adult uses her formal name instead of "Mommy." The adult says, "Well, I'll fix you! I'm going to tell Mrs. Andrew H. Boswell, Jr., on you!" When the child gleefully challenges again, the adult can use her familiar name and say, "Well, I'm going to tell Dena on you! So there!" The adult can take the list of personal terms that exclusively identify her to great lengths and say, "Well, then I'm going to tell the woman with all the kids who lives in the white house on you!"

Box and Sheet It
Companionship or Opposite Game of Adventure

This make-believe game requires several sheets, a big box, and imagination. Since the children are elementary age, the box should be refrigerator size if possible.

"OK, everybody in now?" calmly asks the father as he and the children settle comfortably into the big box in the middle of the living room floor.

"Well, Mateys, we have a long and dangerous voyage ahead of us now," he says with an accent as if he has become a seagoing crewman awaiting the brave captain's next command. "Ahoy. Ship ahoy, Sir!" he adds, singling out one child as leader.

"Should I hoist the sails, Cap'n, and weigh the anchor, Sir?" the father inquires so as to coax his child's creative thinking.

"Blimey! The wind's contrary and the anchor's heavy!" he exclaims as he stands up in midship and fans the sheet as if it were a big white sail and pretends to pull up the anchor.

As the sheet settles down over the box, the father and the children stretch out as if sleeping on the hard wooden deck of their vessel. Someone keeps watch, always peeking out from the sheet to see if the feared sea dragon is swimming after them.

"To your feet, Mateys! We've run aground!" excitedly yells the father after suddenly bumping against the box walls as if the ship hit a rocky shore.

"Cap'n, she's taking water! Is it overboard with us, or do we repair the hole?" he asks in a frightened and quivering voice.

At this point in the voyage, any number of imaginative events could happen. For example, the ship never really hit anything. Rather, a blue whale bumped into it! The friendly talking whale agrees to pull their damaged vessel into port if they rope his tail. Or the battered ship is really going down! High waves are crashing against the ship's sides. A howling wind is flapping the canvas sails. "Man overboard! Man overboard!" yells the father as he pretends to fall out of the ship and begins to tip the box.

The box and sheet it game was role-played as if the box and sheets were a sea vessel. They could have just as easily become a spaceship, a playhouse, or a barn.

Treasure Chest for Children
Companionship or Opposite Game of Adventure

The children want to play dress up and decide to pull out the big storage box containing Mom's prom dress, Daddy's outdated suit and ties, and a whole lot of other stuff.

Every child should experience the joy of a rummage box of old grown-up clothes and things. Outdated high heels, ragged garden gloves, old straw hats and caps, costume jewelry, Mom's ancient prom dress, and Dad's frayed black suit and tie are all marvelous costumes to fuel the child's imagination in creative play.

"I'm the mommy and you're the daddy," decides the six-year-old as she pulls the faded chintz gown from the dress-up chest. Struggling with the scratchy lining, she finally gets it over her head and zipped up the back.

"Heee! Heee! Look! Daddy's coat touches the floor!" says her ten-year-old sister as she buttons the jacket and knots the threadbare red tie around her neck.

"Our house is the couch," they decide and walk arm in arm through the family room where their mother is dusting the furniture.

"Well, who are you?" she asks, observing their impersonation of herself and her husband.

"We're the grown-ups who live here!" respond the children with seriousness as they walk with exaggerated and dignified steps to the couch.

"Oh, Mr. and Mrs. Boswell, I didn't know you would be returning so soon! I'm so sorry the housework isn't completed!" suddenly exclaims the mother who has become Frieda, the newly arrived housekeeper from Europe.

"Is there anything I can get you, Mr. and Mrs. Boswell? Perhaps the newspaper, a drink of milk, some cookies? Ah, you and your lovely family are so kind." With a flurry, Frieda dusts off the table in front of the children and, in her excitement, begins dusting them.

"Heee! Heee! Mommy, don't do that! It tickles!" respond the children as they push away the feathery duster.

"Oh, dear! I don't know what's come over me! One minute I think I'm Frieda, the housekeeper, and the next, your mommy! Dear, dear, dear, what am I to do?" the mother half mutters in bewilderment as she leaves the family room heading for the kitchen.

"I know what I'll do! If you really are Mr. and Mrs. Boswell, please come to the kitchen and I will serve you a snack."

Creative play arising from the treasure chest for children game allows the parent to be either a friendly companion or a friendly antagonist toward the children. This feature is also true in the box and sheet it game.

In the role play, Frieda was a playful antagonist—she positioned herself under the authority of her make-believe employers and then playfully aggravated them by tickling with the feather duster. The children could say, "Stop," request playful obedience from the mother, and demonstrate kindness to the housekeeper from Europe.

The adult could just as easily become Frieda the playful companion. She could impersonate the sweet make-believe visiting sister of Mrs. Boswell or become Frederick, one of Mr. Boswell's business associates.

The adult could dress up with the children as well as pretend an impersonation. She could put on some of the old treasure chest items or creatively use the objects surrounding her at the time.

Both the box and sheet it game and the treasure chest for children game are to be viewed as brief reprieves from your busy work schedule. A longer, more concentrated time may be given to the games if you choose; however, usually five or ten minutes are more than adequate to spellbind your youngster and join him in a creatively playful activity.

Hideaway Peeking
Companionship Game of Adventure

Children need special individualized attention from their parents. When there are several children in a family, the adult needs to be sure to routinely practice a getaway time with each child.

This game is a more advanced version of the household hideout companionship game in chapter 12. More intrigue, imagery, and mystery are involved, and the child participates more as a conspiring accomplice.

"Shhh! Let's see if anyone misses us!" suspiciously whispers the mother as she secretly calls to her eight-year-old daughter. Together, they attempt to slip away during an active, though nonstressful, family time (during a relaxed Saturday afternoon when the mother's absence would be missed but not critically, like at mealtime).

"Keep on the lookout, but try to act normal so no one will notice us!" instructs the mother, and holding her daughter's hand, she tiptoes quickly to a large piece of furniture, looks around to see if all is clear, and hides under the dining room table.

"Whew, we made it!" sighs the mother in relief once they are comfortably settled.

"What are we doing?" asks the child the first time. (Afterward, the youngster will delightfully join in the make-believe adventure.)

"Well, you see, it was time for me to get away from all my work for a little while and have some fun, and I wanted you to be with me. Let's be real quiet and peek out to see what everyone is doing." The mother acts like a scout surveying the terrain and reports back what she sees the family doing. (She describes their activity if she can see them or make believes what they may be doing if she can't.) She encourages her child to join in the scouting activity. She accentuates the thrill and excitement of not being discovered—yet.

"I think all's clear for a while. Let's take a break, OK? Here, you hold the flashlight and I'll read the story." The mother and the child snuggle closely, heads touching, enjoying a special hideaway time together. Whether discovered or not by the others, the adventure time is to end pleasantly. (If discovered prematurely, include others as welcomed reinforcements rather than exclude them as annoying intruders.)

"OK, I guess it's time to go back. We'll get away again sometime. Sure was fun being together! I love you." The mother and the child slip out from behind their hiding place, trying not to be seen or discovered, sharing the secret and mystery of a special time away.

Candy in the Closet
Companionship Game of Endearment

This game is similar to hideaway peeking except for the central feature of food. Just as you may confide privately in your best friends over a cup of coffee, so you speak privately with your child over a shared treat. Children usually do not like coffee so an appropriate substitute must be made.

Sharing a small handful of colorful M&M's in a bedroom closet can communicate a really special meeting place for a child. It is where the little heart more readily may unload a concern, share a joy, tell a secret. Because the place and activity are out of the ordinary, the adult also seems less the normal parental self and more a special person. The atmosphere conveys, "This is our special hideout as confidants!" Tasty food feeds more than the tummy; it feeds the child's spirit as well.

Bat Legs and Lizards
Opposite Game of Endearment

This game teaches childlike gratitude in a playfully creative way.

"What's for snack, Mommy?" is the repeated cry of hungry little children. Sometimes what is offered is met with childish disappointment because it is not their favorite treat or it is not cold, hot, or sweet enough.

"What's for snack?" repeats the mother as if startled that the children would really want to know. "Well, you know, your favorite!" hedges the mother as if trying to put off answering her children's question. She may pretend to be trying to avoid looking them in the eye; she may cover up the mixing bowl with her hand as if to hide from them what is really inside; she may even say under her breath, "I sure hope they don't ask me that again!"

"Come on, Mommy! What's for snack?" insist the children.

"OK! OK! You really want to know! We're having bat legs and lizards! That is what's for snack!"

"Nawww! Mom, what's really for snack?" clamor the children, not for one moment believing their mother's teasing answer.

"I told you! Bat legs and lizards!" repeats the mother with an impish smile at offering something the children would truly dislike.

"Or I could fix rhinoceros skins instead!" the mother thoughtfully adds to tease her youngsters a bit more.

"Mommm! Come on! You're just kidding us! You're not cooking bat legs or lizards or rhinoceros skins really!"

"I'm not? Well, you're right. I'm just making plain old chocolate chip cookies. Maybe I'll make bat legs tomorrow," she contemplates out loud as the children seem a little relieved and pleased that their snack is cookies.

Hatching
Opposite Game of Adventure

Often a child's simple misbehavior arises from a need for attention. From boredom to being too full of energy, many times a child's misbehavior is merely his childish attempt to be loved, noticed, or included by someone, usually the parent.

Set a rambunctious child down on the couch and begin this playful dialogue: "You've been so full of energy today that I think you need to be hatched! That's what I think!"

"What is that?" asks the child.

"When little girls or little boys get full of energy, they need to get the energy hatched out of them," explains the mother with mock seriousness.

"Like little eggs that are hatched properly, little children are tickled until they say, 'Peep, peep, peep,'" says the mother as she begins to playfully tickle her child. If the child peeps immediately, the mother pronounces that the child is hatched properly.

Sometimes a child will hold off peeping for as long as possible. The mother adds a fun twist to the game by saying, "Of course, you know that little boys are to say 'cock-a-doodle-doo,' and little girls are to say 'cluck, cluck, cluck,' to be hatched properly?" The child will likely reverse the proper response, and the mother will pretend added frustration over her girl crowing or her boy clucking.

The playful romp leaves the child physically tired, emotionally satisfied, and happily victorious. All are important factors in helping to promote more family love, peace, and unity.

Stop Growing! You Didn't Get My Permission!
Opposite Game of Endearment

Being mischievous is second nature with the family. Good mischief adds a special touch of affection, which bonds the children more closely with their parents.

This opposite game is similar to the tickle me to sleep game in chapter 11 and may be used with very young as well as elementary-age children. The emphasis is on the child not getting parental permission in regard to some outrageous and impossible event.

"My, you're getting sooo big!" observes the mother, letting out the cuffs in her nine-year-old son's pants.

"I think you may have grown one whole inch this summer!" she exclaims rather proudly and hugs her little boy, who feels rather proud of such a big accomplishment, too.

"Yes, you're growing into quite a big boy!" she repeats while pulling out the last few hem threads on his trousers.

"But wait, you didn't get my permission to grow up!" the mother suddenly thinks out loud and looks with a pretended startled expression at her son.

"You're getting to be a big boy without my permission!" she continues and may pretend to be getting really upset about the situation.

"Why, if you keep growing, you'll be a man someday! I won't have my precious little boy anymore! You better stop this growing up right this very minute!" she exclaims, working herself up to a playful frenzy.

"I just won't have it!" she sputters as if to settle the matter once and for all.

The nine-year-old relishes the advantage he experiences over his mother. He is doing exactly the opposite of his mother's pretend wishes, and there is nothing she can do about it!

Olympic Dishwashing Contest
Companionship Game

The children have work assignments throughout the summer days. The mother wants the children to learn that work can be enjoyable and even fun. Adding a creative touch to routine and sometimes monotonous household chores can make a real difference.

The normal household chores involve food, clothes, dishes, and cleaning. This companionship game focuses on washing dishes.

"Yes! Yes! Yes! We're in!" exclaims the mother with energy and excitement to the children who are helping to clean off the kitchen table after dinner.

"In what?" questions one child as she stacks the scraped dinner plates on the counter.

"What! Why, the Olympic Dishwashing Contest! We qualified as finalists!" says the mother proudly and squirts liquid dish soap into the sink filling with warm sudsy water.

"We're two points behind the Czechs. But if we finish these dishes in under ten minutes, we could win the gold! Hurry, grab a towel and get ready to dry!" she explains.

With an official lift of her hand, the mother exclaims, "On your mark! Get set! Go!" and flashes down her hand as if flagging the race to begin.

"Hurry! Quick! Be careful not to break anything. We'll lose two points!" are all in-character verbal challenges to do the job well and fast.

As the children scamper to dry and put away the dishes, the mother gazes out the kitchen window as if overseeing the contest and makes interesting comments to spur on her little Olympic contestants: "Oh, no, the Japanese are two dishes ahead! Ahhh, the Czechs dropped a fork! The German dishwasher got soap in his eyes!"

Just before the last dish is washed, dried, and put away, the mother exclaims, "I think we're going to make it. I think we've, yes, yes, we've won the gold medal! We're the new dishwashing Olympic gold medal winners!" The mother and the children dance with excited hysteria at winning such a prestigious award.

(Our children once became so involved with the make-believe, they instantly placed their hands over their hearts and began singing the national anthem and waving to the crowd! It was an Olympic year, and they had seen our athletes do that.)

Cash Register the Dishes Away
Companionship Game of Adventure

When our middle daughter was a teenager, she came up with this one while baby-sitting some young elementary-age children.

"Let's clean up the kitchen for your mommy and daddy, OK?" our daughter suggested to the two little boys after dinner.

"Nooo! We don't want to wash dishes!" was their obvious and predictable response.

"Oh, but these aren't dishes. They're make-believe money, and we have to put all the cash away!" she explained. "You see, the glasses are five-dollar bills, the plates are one-dollar bills, the knives are quarters, the forks are dimes, and the spoons are nickels. We have to put the money away in the bank drawers before closing time! Come on! Let's get started!"

Racing to get the plates and glasses on the shelves and the silverware correctly arranged in the drawer, the two little boys asked if they could help wash the dishes all over again and play the game a second time.

First Pick
Opposite Game of Endearment

Make-believe games can teach profound moral values.

"I want that one!" said the six-year-old as her older sister reached for the big round chocolate chip cookie just cooled down for eating.

"No! I get it! Mommy, I touched it first!" countered the big sister as she secured the perfectly shaped one on the counter.

"What about that cookie?" the mother asked, pointing to a misshapen smaller one a little burnt around the edges.

"No! We don't want that one!" responded both children with a frown.

"Who will pick the different one first?" the mother gently asked the children while continuing to spatula up a fresh cooked batch from the oven. "Different cookies have as much feelings as the others. They are special and need love, too. Suppose you were different in some way. Would you want people to frown and turn away from you?"

The children paused to think how sad and lonely to be treated differently from the rest.

"I want the little brown one," quietly spoke up the big sister, who is an especially tenderhearted child. "It's my first pick."

What fascinating moral lessons for life can you weave around a burnt cookie? This same regard for different people can move a child in real life to stand up for them and defend their rights.

Sharing Their World

The busy summer day comes to a close. All the little children are tucked into bed and are falling asleep. Their day was filled with memorable close interaction with parents who deeply care for and love them. The parents expressed their affection and friendship in a language the children heard and understood, and the children responded with love.

The elementary-age ones especially were drawn closer by their folks identifying with them in a fun-filled way. Sharing their world of growing up, making it a little easier for the children to want to emulate them, the adults have gained an invaluable access to each child's heart and life. Capturing the heart in a loving relationship will become more of a reality. As the parents continue expressing their love in creative and playful ways, the child is won over more completely for a lifetime.

The elementary age soon passes, you all too quickly face an adolescent, and the dynamics of your relationship change. Creative play becomes a familiar remembrance of childhood, a subtle emotional connection between you and your child that still unites you as best friends even though the child is growing to adulthood.

Parents of adolescents may wonder whether creative play builds relationships in these later years if not practiced consistently in the younger years. The dynamics of creative play to touch a child's or an early adolescent's heart and move him to a closer relationship remain the same. Creative play is for a lifetime, and those who communicate through it will experience emotional bonding regardless of age.

CHAPTER 14

Creative Make-Believe for an Adolescent

"Your hair is silky, and you don't have wrinkles. I know it can't be helped," teases the mom to her thirteen-year-old daughter as they brush their hair together in the bathroom. She sincerely states several positive qualities about her daughter and then playfully reverses the expected comments about the qualities.

"Actually, I know you wish your hair was graying and your skin was more wrinkled like mine, but that's life," continues the mom, staging a mock rivalry in which she is actually affirming and complimenting her daughter's commendable qualities by playfully comparing them to her own qualities.

"Oh, Mom, come on. You know you're kidding!" responds the teenager, who is inwardly pleased by her mother's affirmation and thankful to be the loser in the contest.

"Sweetheart, just because your hair is shiny and silky and your skin is soft doesn't mean you should wish to look like your thirty-eight-year-old mom!" the adult continues. "What can I say? When you've got some gray hair and wrinkles, you've just got them!" playfully flaunts the mother as if boasting about aging.

This opposite game communicates basic messages of love, acceptance, and friendship to a growing teen who might otherwise have difficulty in hearing and believing such adult sentiments. The mother expressed sincere admiration. The teen felt greater self-worth because her good qualities were complimented and lovingly singled out. Best friends appreciate each other. Sincere affirmation was expressed with a playful twist. Why go to the trouble?

Most adolescents question and challenge their world and their parents' views. The adult says it is white; the teen says it is black. The parental "Yes, you will" statement may lead to the teenager's "No, I won't" attitude and response. Had the adult said, "You are pretty; your hair is shiny, and your skin is soft," the teen probably would flatly deny believing or accepting such parental affirmation. "No, I'm ugly; I hate my hair, and my face is pimply" would be a more likely response.

Creative play alleviates much of the built-in contest between adult and child. The growing child may counter all he wishes in creative play; yet he experiences a wholesome aspect of winning in the relationship. Sensing sweet victory without truly defying the parent, he is drawn closer as a good friend to his parent.

Creative play may communicate companionship without the reverse feature occurring within the game. The teen needs to be taken seriously, to be regarded with growing equality in the relationship. This is a tangible signal that the adult regards the teen as a good companion, maturing and becoming more equal. Creative play offers ways for the teen to appropriately experience equality in game form, which helps to satisfy and defuse her grab for it in real life.

A maturing youngster naturally resists being treated as a child, though the actions may be truly childish. An adult may confuse the youngster's need to continue being childlike while maturing with his need to discard childish practices. Correcting the child's energetic *childlike* expressions may become mixed with proper parental correction of *childish* antics. Helping the youngster to grow up includes enhancing the former and discouraging the latter.

How can you be playful with someone who desperately wants to be taken seriously? Master becoming playfully creative with your teen in imaginative games that are fun and show adult regard for the child's growing maturity. To successfully bridge the generational gap, keep in mind general guidelines when playing with an adolescent.

Creative Play Bridges the Gap

You need to continually attempt good relational communication as we've discussed throughout this book. Good friends together playing a fun activity or good friends playfully pitting themselves against each other in mock rivalry must underlie the interaction. Unresolved problems, hidden negative messages, and true rivalry heighten animosity between parent and child, and no amount of creative play will remove the destructive effect on a relationship.

The factor of finally becoming adultlike in thought, skill, and size alone triggers a more mature direction for the adolescent (age eleven through late teens). Both adolescent and adult are capable of confusing childlike with childish behavior and rejecting creative playfulness as immature and beneath them. By engaging in a playful verbal or physical romp, the adult signals that he esteems youthful expression and wants to encourage it in his growing teenager.

A teen's fragile sense of dignity must be regarded in real life as well as in creative play. A strong sense of affirmation must underlie your words and actions. Your sensitivity to appropriate issues about which to playfully tease is crucial. Creative play applauds, cheers, and uplifts a youngster's self-worth. It helps to diminish rather than fan the natural uncertainty and negative feelings of the adolescent years. An adolescent is especially sensitive about looks and abilities. Creative play lovingly helps her to lighten up and not take things so seriously; it reassures her that her maturity is not being ridiculed or disregarded, just lovingly engaged in a playful manner. You give your child an avenue to express her kid side while keeping her mature side.

Use your teen's natural physical quality of contesting in a creative, positive way. Blend nonthreatening challenges or comparisons with a childlike spiritual demeanor. The mother in the gray hair and wrinkles opposite game contested her daughter's hair and complexion while at the same time sincerely complimenting her. Your genuineness in being playfully childlike and using the physical quality of contesting in a positive manner will determine how well your teen hears and receives the compliment.

Overstating, understating, and reversing the desired obvious are the best way to spellbind a teenager. They add a playful twist that catches the adolescent off guard. Maturity adds a new dimension: you help your teenager remember and express childlikeness.

Teenagers in the Household

Through creative play, you can exchange fun, friendship, and vital heart messages with your growing child. The relationship can be tremendously strengthened by playfully identifying with your youngster. How do you seize the moment of playful creativity and build lasting unity? Let's see how it is done.

When the youngest child turned six, there were also two teenagers (seventeen, sixteen), two early teens (fourteen, thirteen), one preteen (twelve), and an eight-year-old in the household. Two parents tried to capture the children's hearts in a loving relationship toward Christ and within the family. Creative play greatly facilitated this objective. Peek in on a week's worth of make-believe games that positively affected the teenagers.

Snuggle In, Curl Up
Companionship Game of Endearment

An older child needs to experience parental companionship in quiet, nondemanding ways. Before rising or going to bed is an excellent time to approach a teenager in the spirit of a good companion. Sitting on the edge of the bed or stretching out in opposite directions while talking communicates to the parent and the child a feeling of closeness.

"Time to get up, Miss Sleepy Head," pleasantly calls the mother as she enters the teenager's bedroom.

The child's obvious reluctance is complete as she pulls the sheet over her head and moans, "Mom, I don't want to get up."

Instead of badgering or issuing ultimatums, the mother snuggles under the blanket and gently rubs her sleepy daughter's forehead. Or she may scratch her back. Or the mother may choose not to touch her daughter at all, just curl up close and whisper, "I love you, Sweetheart," in her ear. Remaining quietly near for a few minutes as the child stirs to awareness communicates good companionship. Using terms of endearment adds to the warmth of the moment.

Hero for the Day
Companionship or Opposite Game of Endearment

This make-believe game communicates a parent's thankful and praising reaction for the teenager's positive effort in carrying out a responsibility.

"Great job, Son!" compliments the father as he examines the freshly washed and waxed car in their driveway.

"I really appreciate your getting the job done," he sincerely thanks the sixteen-year-old and hands him his allowance for the week.

"You're my hero for the day!" he adds with a playful touch. "If it weren't for your washing our car, I'd be out here scrubbing it! Thanks, Big Guy, for a great job."

Being someone's hero for the day is a playful and pleasant affirmation of friendship. Wanting a hero and being a hero to someone are felt needs a person experiences, and it is pleasing to be classified as a hero, even in the context of play.

As an opposite game, becoming a hero by washing a car reverses the parent's becoming a hero to the child. "I honor your help, industry, and care in behalf of our family" is the sincere tribute being given in the context of creative play.

You Won the Award
Opposite Game of Adventure

The trash is bulging the kitchen garbage container again. The sixteen-year-old son forgot to empty the trash last night and left for school in a rush this morning. The mother decides to make a point without nagging or taking it out herself.

While relaxing in his bedroom listening to music, the teenage son hears a knock.

"May I come in?" politely asks the mother.

"Sure, Mom," he responds.

"I'm so proud of you, Sweetheart!" she compliments with bubbly enthusiasm.

"About what?" wonders her son.

"About the award you get, Dear!" she excitedly responds.

"What award?" he asks with bewilderment and growing curiosity.

"The prize in the kitchen for you," states the mother.

"Where? I didn't see any prize," he counters.

"You will. Come on, I'll show you," she says.

Entering the kitchen together, she lifts the plastic bag from the garbage container and proudly awards her son the huge prize of taking out the trash. "You won the award! No need to thank me. It's all yours, Sweetheart," she playfully congratulates him.

The son probably won't be taken in a second time. No problem. The adult simply delivers the prize to the teenager.

Make a playful ceremony of awarding the youngster an armload of folded clothes to put away, a plastic bag of trash to carry out, a pile of dirty clothes for the hamper, wet bath towels to be hung up, or the dirty dishes left in the bedroom.

Follow the "You won the award" congratulation with the instruction to properly attend to duties and responsibilities. The point of being playfully aggressive in a work assignment defuses your aggravation in waiting long periods of time for the job to be done. It initially confronts your teen in a more friendly manner regarding laziness, forgetfulness, or unwillingness to help. Use a creative avenue to begin the confronting process.

Mirror TV Interview
Companionship Game of Adventure

Family members in the same household share each other's space, common ground, and mutually held items. Teenagers tend to be more reclusive, private, and possessive of themselves and their things. Make the most of any family overlap by creatively relating.

Appropriate occasions arise when parent and teenager are together in front of a large mirror. Combing hair, applying makeup, shaving, examining the fit of a dress, and adjusting a tie are common occurrences shared by family members.

The father scratches his tangled hair and rubs his stubbled chin as he stares half awake into the bathroom mirror. His twelve-year-old daughter knocks on the door to borrow the toothpaste. Handing her the tube, he hugs her and draws her in front of the mirror.

"Ladies and gentlemen, I want to introduce to you the finest twelve-year-old girl in the world. This talented young lady can take the scruffy wreck standing before you and transform—I mean literally transform—her poor old dad into a clean-shaved and combed man by one little kiss on the cheek!"

Talking with pretend seriousness, the father adds, "Daughter, do you have a word for the audience before accomplishing this amazing feat?" Putting his arm around her shoulders and standing in front of the mirror, he holds his toothbrush up as if it's a microphone.

The daughter's response may be pleasant and positive or withdrawn and negative. Her response is not the adult's focus. If positive, the father hams it up with creative inventions and comments that imitate a live interview. He says, "Thank you. Now for a two-minute station break." And he proceeds to mimic a commercial about Bubbly Brand toothpaste that is everybody's favorite and demo a bubbly tooth brushing. He hands his toothbrush microphone to his daughter. He exclaims, "The moment has arrived! The kiss that transforms me will now be given!" and acting as if looking into a camera, he stares at the mirror while leaning sideways to be kissed.

The daughter's response may be withdrawn and negative. She may roll her eyes, act disgusted, and walk away. The father ends his playful attempt with a pleasant, teasing comment. "I may look like a scruffy, messy-haired father today because I didn't get a kiss from my favorite twelve-year-old daughter!" he calls after her from the bathroom door. He has playfully communicated significance to his daughter. She is special and affects her daddy's life.

Professor Viggle Bomb
Companionship Game of Endearment

A fictitious family hero or villain adds novelty and creativity to the household, especially with preteens. Leaving behind many younger games, the preteen enjoys an outrageous and playful romp that uses a third party. Focusing on a third party downplays the emphasis on the adolescent, allowing her to safely participate almost as an understudy. The individual may be personified by a family member, or the individual may remain an imaginary third party. The hero may be eccentric, the villain rascally; yet both demonstrate some positive qualities in creative play.

The fictitious hero or villain is dramatized best through companionship games. The make-believe character may identify with the family's history or traits or be imagined as totally different from family members. The character is named with a term of endearment.

Professor Viggle Bomb is the friendly family physician who oversees the younger members' personal hygiene: flossing teeth, trimming nails, removing splinters from fingers and knots from hair. He speaks with an accent. He is gentle and knowledgeable, though he acts confused and disoriented most of the time. Either parent may impersonate him.

"Is time we clean the teeth, yes?" reminds the mother before the youngsters head for bed. "Professor Viggle Bomb expects pearly white chompers, so we must get started," she continues while handing six-inch threads of floss to each child.

"Hold the string like so and we clean between each tooth! Is good!" remarks the mother as she helps wind floss securely around fingers to reach the difficult back ones.

Her twelve-year-old frays the floss in a back molar, snapping the thread lodged tightly between two teeth. "Mom, it hurts! It won't come out!" the youngster complains.

"Professor Viggle Bomb to the rescue!" the mother exclaims, instructing the preteen to lie flat on the bed with mouth wide open. "Surgery may be necessary!" the mother dramatizes as she winds a long thread around each pointer finger and begins flossing the back molar.

"Is bad. I will extract it—pull it out with pliers!" she playfully continues while gently working on the child's tooth. "Always my victims . . . patients survive!" she concludes, lifting out the stubborn floss.

Big Max Is Back!
Companionship Game of Endearment

Big Max is a pesky overseer who loves to catch people not doing their jobs. He may show up any time, day or night, demand to inspect a person's work, and report the person to the Big Boss. If that happens, treats, privileges, and rewards may be forfeited. When a Big Max sighting occurs, the adult and the youngsters race to complete a work project so that he never finds the job undone.

"Time to fold clothes, you two!" announces the mother as she drops a load of clothes warm from the dryer right on top of her two teens resting in the family room.

"Ahhh, Mom! We don't want to fold them," they respond simultaneously.

"Well, I don't want to, either. So, let's do them together fast!" she suggests and sits down among the strewn clothes.

"One does the towels, I'll do the underthings, and the other the shirts and shorts," she offers, dividing up the work. "Hurry! You know Big Max might come and spoil everything!" she reminds them, pretending grave concern. "He said if everything isn't put away in five minutes, we'll fold the next load instead of someone else!"

Rallying the workers, the mother moves frantically to complete her portion of the work assignment. "He's coming! I hear his truck in our driveway! Hurry!" she says in breathless alarm.

All clothes are folded, and now begins the dash to put them away: "Quick! He's at the door! I hear him knocking!" Rushing past the closet door, the mother sharply knocks on it before putting away her pile.

"He's here!" the mother exclaims as if beside herself with apprehension and loudly urges her youngsters to quickly put up the clothes and meet back in the family room.

Breathlessly rejoining her teenagers, the mother stretches out on the couch and pronounces the family safe from Big Max, who finally left the premise one minute ago.

Wanna Swap?
Opposite Game of Endearment

Teenagers and preteens focus on their appearance with critical intensity. Creative play may help them to lighten up and accept imperfections as a normal part of life. Help your teen refocus and examine and appreciate positive qualities instead of seeing only perceived or real negative qualities.

Staring in the bedroom mirror, the teenage daughter blots her light pink lipstick and examines a pimple on her chin. With disgust she adds a fresh dab of cover-up. She feels doomed in the blemished stage of adolescence!

"May I borrow your hair dryer?" requests the mother standing in the doorway.

"Go ahead. It won't do me any good!" replies the daughter despondently.

"What's wrong, Sweetheart?" asks the mother, sitting on the bed beside her daughter.

"I'm ugly!" sums up the teenager.

"Wanna swap?" suggests the mother.

"Swap what?" questions the daughter with suspicion.

"I'll swap you my wrinkles, gray hair, extra pounds—all my uglies—for what makes you feel ugly," gently suggests the mother as she lists some of her imperfections. "You can be older like me and not have as much energy. I'll get to be younger and have that cute little nose of yours and your pretty bright eyes! I'll get to have those dimples—I love dimples—and your smaller shoe size! Hey! I like this idea. Let's swap!"

The adult selects admirable and desirable characteristics of the child, compares them to less-desirable physical qualities the parent possesses, then verbally tallies up the two lists in a make-believe game of swapping. As the teenager faces the reality of another's physical imperfections, tolerance and acceptance of her own are encouraged.

Building Strong Family Ties

The week of make-believe at the Boswell residence comes to a close. The adolescents of the household feel affirmed and regarded as maturing adults while at the same time remaining playful, growing youngsters. The healthy emotional connection between parent and adolescent is strengthened as a result of experiencing fun and laughter and creatively sharing life's lessons. Because the parents were approachable and playful, the teenagers are encouraged to open their hearts more willingly and reveal their true selves.

The years of adolescence will witness the continued building of strong family ties. The teenage heart is still receptive to being touched by playful creativity and won over to a more loving relationship. The adolescent stage is still open to the imaginative touches of the parent who deeply cares.

Conclusion:
Connect Hearts
for a Lifetime

C reative play is a language communicating to the heart of a child at any age. Your time, effort, and energy are bountifully rewarded with a loving and lasting relationship. Capturing your child's heart is like creating a delicate work of art by loving patience, forethought, and precision. Communicating with childlike maturity will encourage your child's receptivity to you, to the relationship, and to your values. Some of the best-loved memories and most lasting lessons occur during treasured times when you creatively communicate with your youngster. Capture the moments of childhood now, and you are more likely to connect with your child for a lifetime.